HUNGER FOR MORE IN LIFE

JD

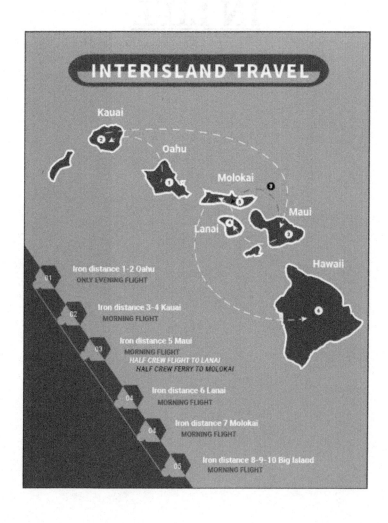

Dedication

My son, you have such a strong presence that fills me with joy. Although I am still learning to raise you, I strive to ensure your life is filled with knowledge and understanding.

This book is a testament to our journey together and some of the obstacles I faced to be where I am today. I hope it will give you the motivation and guidance to pursue your dreams and ambitions. You must always remember that the path you take in life is yours alone, and only you have the power to make the best decisions for yourself.

My biggest wish is that you remain curious and hungry to grow. Do not be afraid of the unknown but use it as an opportunity to gain experience and explore.

Noah, my love for you is immeasurable. I am so proud of the young man you are becoming and will continue to be. No matter what life brings, I will always be there, loving you. As we used to say: *"I love you today."*

Daddy loves you, Noah!

Acknowledgments

I thank those random strangers I encountered along the way that reminded me that life is unpredictable and full of surprises and serendipity. Although it was not the help I anticipated, their support allowed me to overcome my challenges and reach my goals. It is a lesson that I carry with me to this day. I have learned that regardless of how difficult the journey may seem, there is always a way to get where you want to go with the help of unexpected allies.

When I look back at the people that have supported me in my journey, it is hard to believe how far I have come. Pierre-marc Gagnon gave me hope when I was ready to give up on everything. Oscar Compean became like a brother while being my photographer.

Despite his beliefs, my dad worked hard to show me love. I am extremely grateful for Joe Jaffe's belief in me and Jeff Schiller's friendship and coaching. I am thankful for Christine Cogger, who believed in me at a crucial moment in my life. Emeka was like a brother from another mother, supporting me through it all.

I owe a great deal to Michelle, Sara, Shane, Packo and Miriam, who have been with me every step of the Epicdeca. Specialized Canada and Precision Fuel & Hydration deserve special mention for their support and encouragement.

These people showed me through actions that it is possible to go further in life. I am grateful for them every day and will forever remember their contribution to my growth.

Thank you all!

Disclaimers

It is important to remember that the claims I make in this book should not be taken as gospel. While they may be informed by research and my experiences, I cannot guarantee their accuracy. Therefore, use your judgment to think critically even if you agree with my arguments.

Everyone's background, education, experience, and work ethic are unique. What works for me may not necessarily yield the same results for you. Your journey will be different, and you will have to face the consequences of your actions. The path to success is never guaranteed, but hard work and dedication may bring you closer to your desired outcome.

This book is intended for informational and educational purposes; it is not intended to substitute for professional medical advice, diagnosis, and/or treatment. Please consult your medical professional before making changes to your diet, exercise routine, medical regimen, lifestyle, and/or mental health care.

About the Author

My name is JD Tremblay. I am a Canadian man filled with courage and conviction. The traumas I experienced in my childhood and military career have been difficult to overcome. However, they have also been instrumental in providing me with an invaluable source of wisdom and strength for the rest of my life. I believe that when we face our fears, take responsibility for our circumstances, and strive to make something out of our lives; we can overcome adversities and create a life of meaning and purpose.

I discovered that taking part in triathlons has immensely benefited my mental and physical health.

As such, I have taken on some of the most grueling triathlons in the world, pushing myself to my limits and beyond. From high-altitude runs to the infamous Epicdeca, I have faced countless challenges with determination and dedication.

As a newly graduated engineer, my technical knowledge and analytical skills have been instrumental in helping me achieve my objectives. However, I believe that the right attitude and a will to succeed can take you further than any theoretical claim or physical strength.

As a father, I have learned the importance of setting an example for my child — an illustration of hard work, humility, and balance. I strive to be a role model for him and demonstrate that no matter what life throws at you, there is always a way to achieve your goals and make the best out of any situation.

Preface

The Epicdeca challenge was an excellent test of self-discipline, determination, and courage. It demonstrated that life is full of demanding situations and that our reactions to them are what define us. It is important to remember that there is no single 'best' way of responding to the challenges we face. Everyone is unique and will have strategies for dealing with problems that arise throughout life's journey.

People should not be discouraged by the fact that there are no winners in an Epicdeca challenge, as these events are designed to encourage us to develop our resilience, patience, and strength of character. Ultimately, it is a reminder that we can all overcome any obstacle if we approach it with the right mindset. Even when things do not turn out exactly as planned, staying positive and learning from our mistakes are important. The Epicdeca challenge is a splendid example of the power of perseverance and can inspire us to become better versions of ourselves.

It was remarkable how, at the end of the day, we all ended up being friends. We had come together as strangers with diverse backgrounds, personalities, and beliefs, yet we managed to connect on a deeper level. In this book, you will find stories of people who made mistakes, failed to respond appropriately, and sometimes even found themselves in precarious situations. What you will also find, however, is how these same people were able to learn from their mistakes and rise above the circumstances. You will also understand that mistakes can be made and still come out on top. You will be inspired to take ownership of your life, understand that everyone has moments of imperfection and make the best of the opportunities that come your way. Only when we embrace our imperfections can we truly learn, grow, and become better people. So, take up this book and read these stories of courage and resilience as you embark on your journey of self-discovery.

The Beginning

Contents

Introduction

"If your goals are not scaring you, set the bar higher."

~JD

It does not matter if you are a lawyer, doctor, engineer, or young professional. Your knowledge may be useless if you do not follow these simple steps. Imagine being in a state of mind where you cannot function or concentrate on your job. It will not matter if you know how to surgically remove half the brain of someone so they can survive. It does not matter if you are a highly-paid professional with years of education and experience. Depression and brain fog can still come for you. What will you do then?

We have all been in a situation where we cannot think straight and need help and guidance to climb out of this seemingly infinite pit. It takes months and years to get out of crippling depression and brain fog so thick that you cannot even think right. At this point, our years of education, material wealth, family, or life have no meaning. What good is it anyway, when you are burnt out beyond capacity, and the only aspect of life that keeps you going is the paycheck at the end of the long and hard month? Where will you find the energy to spend that money and enjoy it? We know what depression is like, but many do not realize that brain fog is also a symptom of depression or severe chronic fatigue. However, brain fog manages to make our lives just as difficult. Brain fog is a condition characterized by forgetfulness, confusion, and a lack of focus or mental clarity. We experience this for many reasons, such as overworking, lack of sleep, stress, and even spending too much time on the computer.

I know this because I have experienced going through all these symptoms of brain fog, which also hinted at the severe depression I had. The medical community generally believes that this condition is caused by high inflammation levels and hormonal changes, which determine our mood, energy, and focus. These severely and sometimes chronically imbalanced hormone levels wreak havoc and chaos in our system, bringing both mental and physical health down.

If left untreated for a long time, brain fog syndrome paves the way for other conditions such as obesity, abnormal menses, and diabetes. For any treatment to work, first, we need to uproot and remove the underlying causes of the issue. Brain fog is typically a direct cause of a lifestyle that does not promote hormonal balance and harmony. A lifestyle deeply entrenched in stress and worry.

In this book, I will share some of the behaviors I have adopted to pull out of this condition. For instance, we sit in front of our computers all day and use mobile phones and tablet devices obsessively, which can cause unhealthy doses of electromagnetic radiation. We take in a lot of unnecessary stress that we may not even be aware of. Did you know any type or level of stress reduces blood flow to the brain, which is why people with chronic stress also often have poor memory? Bad quality of sleep is another reason. To function well, we need a good night's sleep, but people suffering from brain fog often complain of having little to no sleep. Lack of physical activity or exercise may also be a contributing factor.

Healthy eating is particularly important! Someone suffering from brain fog and depression also usually has a bad or unbalanced diet. Additionally, our current environment, brimming with toxins, pollution, chemical substances, and insecticides, also plays a key role in bringing even the strongest person to their knees.

The thing is that mental decline in people is the direct result of poor lifestyle choices and the inability to improve them. Mental decline, followed by physical deterioration, is a common condition and one of the most feared. However, you can help yourself! There are many ways you can maintain better brain function that I will talk about in the subsequent chapters.

While I do not guarantee overnight success, it is still better to seek help as it is the first sign you want to improve. Trust me, sometimes, this is all that it takes. In my years of doing extreme triathlons worldwide, I have learned many valuable life lessons. I am here to share some of this exclusive knowledge with you and help you get back on your feet faster than it took me. Yes, it took me years to get back on my feet and battle depression. But with this invaluable knowledge, it may take you less!

I have lived through many stressful events in my life. However, I will focus on the portion of my life where I acquired the most momentum to get myself out of this misery. This forward motion began when I went to get a college diploma in Construction Engineering. Heck, I even finished at the top of my class. After graduating, I joined a top university in a special program called Integrated Engineering, which included all the different fields of Engineering in one hybrid discipline. I did not enjoy the way the material was taught to us, but I still did my best to complete this program.

My mind was wired differently then, but I hated my life and felt I was not living completely. I wanted a fulfilling life, but where to find one? My debilitating symptoms and low self-esteem prevented me from doing something about it. Even when doing the tasks I was supposed to be doing, which I did not realize until much later, was a part of the cause of my depression and brain fog. It got so bad that I could not even function well or think. Depression is an ugly condition; it takes so much from us, and many years of my life were lost to it. Only the people around me, who knew me, noticed my distress and silent call for help.

Did I get the help I needed? No! I tried to get the help I desperately needed, but I could not. I discovered that most of the people I would reach out to were not prepared to help me. Hence why I created this book. Some of them did not care despite their good words, and the majority were happy it was happening to me and not to them. Unfortunately, this is the way of the world. Many people are so deeply absorbed in their lives that most do not care about others. Even my father, whom I reached out to, did not know how to react to my obvious depression. He could not help me because he, like most people, was never taught how to deal with these situations. It has been some years, but I am happy to announce that my dad has since changed his approach.

At some point, we even fought, which made the situation worse. I remember lying on his couch, looking at the ceiling, not blinking, and completely numb. The minutes would turn into hours and hours into days. The only thing I had going on was that I was breathing, and apparently, it was enough. I cannot even count the number of hours thinking I could not become anyone with a positive future. The level of distress I suffered from believing that others would reject me was beyond my comprehension. I just had to remind myself that I was not enough to get better. This daily reminder was necessary to improve my attitude toward basic tasks.

I was also happy, in a way, that breathing was not a conscious decision. Otherwise, this pragmatic behavior might have stopped my existence. I realized I had been investing my time and energy in the wrong people, which also took a huge toll on my overall health.

I started my journey into triathlon a few years before college. Back then, I had completed only two Sprint triathlons and an Olympic distance. Because I wanted to focus solely on my schooling, I did not compete in a triathlon until years later. While in my senior year of university and at the peak of my depression, I turned to extreme endurance triathlons to cope with the surging number of stressors in my life. Without any form of specific workouts geared toward triathlon, I originally began with a full Ironman in the middle of a summer break from school. At the time, I only challenged myself to be on the start line. I do not recommend this strategy to anyone! I could have seriously injured myself.

However, my depression was so severe that the pain of a full ironman without training was less than the pain I felt inside. The worst part is that no one could even see my distress. Meanwhile, my only goal was to finish the event. Now, I can achieve much larger events because I put in the necessary efforts and actions to reach that stage. I enjoyed the experience of finishing my first Ironman.

Completing this event drove me to do another one two months later. I was sitting in the back of the class, wondering when I would live this experience again. I looked online and registered for another on the same weekend. I went to see the professor after class to tell her I would not be present on Friday. She surprisingly encouraged me to pursue this path and said that she would send me an email with some homework. I got home, put my bike in my vehicle, and drove to Louisville, Kentucky. I slept in a hotel, and for the first time, I was motivated to complete my homework.

When I got back from Kentucky, I registered for my first Ultraman race. I contacted a local running coach to acquire the necessary tool to be confident enough to complete this event. He was happy to put me in contact with a triathlon coach. That evening, I met Jeffrey Schiller, an accomplished cyclist himself who has helped hundreds of athletes achieve their athletic objectives. Our first interview was strange since I did not know the value of my acquired curse, which would eventually turn into a blessing. Because

INTRODUCTION

Jeff was normally only accepting elite athletes, I believed I had no chance of being coached by this man. Nonetheless, he was intrigued by my story and wanted to take part in this journey.

He was one of the first to notice that I was not out to reach a specific outcome, such as going to the Olympics or improving my time on a 5 km run. He immediately noticed that I was on a quest and seeking answers to better myself.

I also admit that I was one of the worst athletes a coach could have. Jeff would put in place a specific training plan, and I would add random races every weekend. His level of patience with me throughout the years has always surprised me. I remember one time he contacted me through social media to see how training was going. I answered that I drove to New York during the school break and was scheduled to race a half marathon on the weekend. Disappointed, he had to talk to me about the necessity of not racing constantly.

With the minimal amount of knowledge I had about my psychological condition, I explained that my mind was broken and needed this mental boost to keep me motivated to live. I would find all sorts of races to keep my mind occupied. One year later, I competed in the Ultraman Canada race. This was the beginning of a new era for me. The challenge consisted of a 10 km swim and 421 km bike ride, followed by a double marathon of 84 km. All of it was over the span of three days and had a 12-hour cutoff time for each day. The most surprising was that the day following each event, I would simply keep training. Even on the days when my coach would schedule a few workouts, I would always end up adding an extra training or two in the day. Jeff and I had many discussions regarding this method. He also understood that my mental health was the principal factor to keep me alive. I was destroying my being, and nothing seemed to be stopping me. This journey eventually led me to the Epicdeca, the longest endurance event that I completed to this date.

The Epicdeca is a challenge that consists of 10 Iron-distance triathlons in 10 consecutive days on all 6 Hawaiian Islands. For those who are not familiar, an Iron-distance is a 3.8 km swim, 180 km bike ride, followed by a 42 km run. The first two iron-distances would be on the island of Oahu. The following two will be conducted on Kauai. Trailed by a single iron-distance on Maui, Lanai, and Molokai in that order. Finally, we would travel to the big island to complete the last three full iron-distances.

The Epicdeca is an ultra-triathlon adventurous experience that, due to challenging logistics, could only accommodate a small group setting of ten athletes worldwide. The race was put in place by the company Epic5, which conducts a Hawaiian race that is half that distance every year.

Only for their tenth anniversary, the company decided to double their annual distance. Some athletes were also registered in the Epic5 challenge and would do the same course as the Epicdeca once we reached the fourth iron-distance. Needless to say, it was the ultimate once-in-a-lifetime experience.

The Epicdeca aims to get people to challenge themselves while going through the beautiful Hawaiian Islands. In fact, many people have completed 10 Iron-distance in 10 days. Most of the time, this is an event that is done on a closed course. However, the difficulty of the Epicdeca challenge was that not only did we have to complete the challenge on a course that was open to traffic but also travel from island to island with a crew of a minimum of four individuals.

Taking part in the Epicdeca challenge also helped my understanding of life and how to get better. While the Epicdeca was not necessarily the sole source of help, my effort and willpower brought me to that stage. What does that tell us? We need to do the work! For example, many people go to university and never find what they want. Yet some find their purpose and calling through these institutions. Ultimately, what matters most is the effort you are willing to put into achieving a desired outcome.

But before this, I was an absolute mess. I destroyed my mind and body to recover from the ordeal my lifestyle choices and unforeseen circumstances had put me through. Instead, I discovered how to recover faster and live healthier for longer. While my parents did not have much money when I was growing up, I still managed to live life fine — or barely — which I was surviving daily. Additionally, my education did not save me from the feelings of low self-esteem and depression I always felt. I did not know what to do about it. Similarly, I kept thinking about life and that I was just one major hurdle away from everything falling apart.

A lot in life is often viewed from an egotistic point of view. We begin to think that our degree, profession, or even money is infallible and will save us from often undesired destructive outcomes of major life events. I am here to tell you that it is hard to escape from the difficulties that will come your way, one way or another. Difficulties will come eventually; how can you prepare to escape from them? You may get overworked, feel down and depressed, and not even have the time to address your basic spiritual, mental, and physical needs. What kind of life is worth living like this?

All research suggests that we now live longer yet do not have healthier habits. We are also not living in a meaningful way as we are meant to live. Many people live to be old, in their late 80s or 90s, but are they living all these years healthy? In fact, many people are not necessarily strong or well. While it may be due to the age factor, it is also due to living a life of stress and unhealthy coping mechanisms.

And to think I was one of those who briefly considered death as the only way out of my miserable existence. Yes, I know; how could I want to end it all just because I had certain traumatic experiences or even may not have certain things in life that other people my age had? My family is not well-connected, nor have they amassed wealth. We never lacked essentials like food, water, or even a roof over our heads. What we did lack was exposure to the sports I wanted to do, as well as basic love and care, which are important aspects of life for a child. Eventually, I figured out that I was tired of being in a perpetual survival mode of the continuous hurdles I would have to overcome.

How Did I Survive?

One of the most important reasons I am alive and well today is that I wanted to survive. I was always constantly hungry for more! I wanted to know more, whether it was knowledge, experience, or anything else. I spent my life always trying my best and looking for opportunities to turn my life around and impact others in the process.

"Life is meant to be a challenge because challenges are what makes you grow."

— Manny Pacquaio

Perhaps the best person to get inspired in life is none other than Manny Pacquaio. A formidable boxing legend yet a humble person. Manny has done so much to turn his life around for the better. Going from a hungry-for-food child to a hungry-for-world title boxing champion. In the process, he has also helped change the fate of his family and other people. Fondly nicknamed PacMan, he is debatably regarded as one of the greatest professional boxers of all time. The man behind the legend has also done amazing things outside of the ring as a humanitarian philanthropist and senator of the Philippines. How did he turn his life around? Through sheer grit, perseverance, resilience, and a deep understanding of his limitations as well as strengths.

Similarly, success for me is defined by being able to complete these events, learn from my mistakes, and impact as many people as possible to understand they can also achieve so much more than their limiting beliefs permit.

For me, life means to be satisfied with what you have achieved but also enjoy the present moment. Especially when an opportunity may arise to surprise your learning process on this journey. Always look forward and see what you can build. Odds are that you may shape something better than you thought could not be possible. Always stay curious and ask questions. Keep your eyes and ears open. Listen and see because you never know what you might learn.

I lived by this motto all my life, even when in the pits of depression. I kept having this urge to challenge myself. I wanted to see how far my ruined mind and body could go before shutting down. I have condensed a solid step process from the lessons I have learned over the years that I applied and tested during the Epicdeca journey. These techniques worked so well that I seized the chance of a lifetime and became one of the world's only three Epicdeca finishers. This achievement was huge in my sight, especially because my family does not have any professional athletes. I certainly did not win the genetic lottery.

Are you already going through dark and painful times? A death in the family, divorce, estrangement, or work stress is getting to you. It could be anything! Remember, the path to healing and recovery took me years to traverse; it might just be a walk in the park for you with the help of this experiential knowledge.

You may wish to find all this knowledge on your own. You may find the path you are looking for, or worse, you may never find it. However, finding it on your own may take years of self-reflection, if not tens of thousands of dollars in therapy sessions. My favorite self-destructive pattern was doing it by myself, free, with random videos that would please my mood when I sporadically had a difficult day.

I would end up retaining little information due to the fact the content was free. I had no commitment and was endlessly searching for answers. I believe this process may assist people in conquering the heaviness in their hearts and returning them to their real thriving selves.

In the following pages, I explain an easy-step process that can be applied to most stressful situations. Additionally, you will find herein knowledge regarding the journey that led me to this triathlon adventure. I have tried to separate both the process and stories to make it easier to depict relevant pieces of the content that is being conveyed. Each chapter will commence with the steps, followed by an associated storyline later in the book. This is done so that this book may be used as a reference without having to go through the entire narrative. I am pleased to share this pain-to-success journey with you. My firsthand experiences and stories are used as an example to show you that success over major depressive conditions can be overcome. If you are not motivated, I hope you are at least entertained. Regardless, I am happy you are reading my first book and encouraging me to grow. While this book is not a medical guide, it can be a great starting point for those who want to explore alternative pathways for improving their health. It offers up a simple yet effective approach that has improved my physical and mental well-being. The information in this book can help provide insight into how our lifestyle choices are connected to our overall health and provide the tools to make changes that can have a positive impact. Of course, it is always important to consult with a healthcare professional before making any major changes to your lifestyle. Taking the time to read this book and reflect on what it teaches can be a fantastic way of learning more about yourself and your health, as well as helping you make better decisions regarding your well-being.

I cannot guarantee your results. However, many people have gone through this process and come out to the other end better than they ever were. The key here is that you need to conduct consistent application of this system. Implement it right away and follow it every day without fail. I would love to hear how this book has transformed your life and if you added your twist to this recipe. Come dive and learn from the tumultuous adventures of this journey that led me to the Epicdeca.

Chapter 1: Mindset

"Design a plan and expect changes."

~JD

Different people have different definitions of success. Some people think success means earning a lot of money, possessions, or respect. Some think having a lot of accomplishments in their career makes them successful in life. No definition is wrong because people have diverse classifications of the same words due to their mindset and life goals.

I think being successful in life means being content and doing all the things you want to do, setting ambitious goals for yourself, and doing your best at every opportunity you decide to undertake. Of course, I think like this because of my mindset, which has changed a lot for the better. Now, I equate my contentment with being successful because it is exceedingly difficult to achieve true success if you are not satisfied with life.

Otherwise, you end up in an endless cycle chasing the next option without valuing your current situation. A strong mindset geared toward success and satisfaction is especially important when achieving anything you set your sight on. It does not even matter how high the fruit on the tree branch is.

What is Mindset?

According to the dictionary definition, mindset is a way of thinking and a mental attitude or inclination. By utilizing this definition, we can derive that if we change our attitude toward a specific desired outcome, our actions will follow suit. Our mindset combines our beliefs, thoughts, emotions, assumptions, and attitudes. These are not just in our conscious thoughts and beliefs but are also present in the subconscious.

Simply put, our mindset guides our life. It encompasses how we view ourselves and makes us think about our place in the world. It also determines what the world is like, around us. This means that having a specific mindset also governs our decisions, choices, and actions according to different situations and environments.

Additionally, it also influences and shapes our outcomes. Obviously, the work we put into making a desired result happen is also important, but having the right mindset will pave the way for success in any endeavor you set your heart on achieving. Unfortunately, having a healthy mindset will not always guarantee success. Some circumstances are beyond our control. However, it is essential to seize an opportunity when it presents itself, which is only possible if we have an inner drive that cannot be satiated.

Hunger Mindset

Concisely, it is an attitude that takes over the mind and body. We spend years of our life trying to build the life we want, but most of the time, we fail. Eventually, we stop trying and just accept our life for whatever it is. This phenomenon is called "learned helplessness." It may be a way that we have seen not produce results for others, or it may be a paradigm that we have witnessed in our life.

Patterns are meant to be shaped by our desired outcome and may not be what they reflect in the current moment. Many times, people lose hope in a situation when it does not work out. When one occasion does not end up as planned, they think the next will also provide a similar outcome. Even if the next condition is not necessarily correlated with the previous. What is paramount is to disconnect both circumstances. It is also imperative to connect good coping mechanisms to allow a healthy forward motion toward your future objectives.

Successful athletes and entrepreneurs know the meaning of being hungry and staying the course. This means all those people did not shy away from the long and arduous journey needed to accomplish something meaningful to them. They had the desire and the drive to accomplish immense and audacious goals. Just imagine what if we had pushed through these psychological barriers sooner, what life could have been. This is the hunger mindset, never stopping despite all odds and always on the lookout for something more, something better.

Over the years, we learn what kind of attitudes and actions have held us back. We note down the

steps that helped us progress closer to the end goal. Just because you stumbled a bit at the beginning of your journey does not mean you have to stop entirely.

What have you learned so far from your life that you could implement today?

Remain Teachable

Teachability is essential for success in life. It allows us to learn from our mistakes and experiences, as well as the wisdom of others. When we remain teachable, we can become open to innovative ideas and ways of thinking that could benefit our lives. When surrounded by supportive people who offer advice, it is important to remain malleable and take in what they have to say. Otherwise, we risk repeating the same patterns of behavior that may not be conducive to our success. It is only by being teachable that we can overcome the obstacles standing in our way and become successful.

It is the same with our hunger for knowledge and growth. If we remain teachable, then it will give us the energy and motivation to keep on going no matter what life throws our way. We can be brave and take responsibility for the choices we make, which will bring us to a better place if we remain teachable. By being exposed to learning, the world opens its arms and offers us a wealth of possibilities. We just need to take that first step and believe that we have what it takes to acquire the anticipated information. Doing so will help us to stay excited and motivated about the journey of life.

Being teachable is an important quality to have, but it is crucial to draw the line between learning from everyone and being foolish. It is important to consider the knowledge of others while also weighing their advice and opinions to ensure it is something worth taking into consideration. Remember that some people may not have the most accurate understanding of a situation, so it is important to take all of this into account before making any decisions.

Attitude

An athlete's attitude is the biggest tool in their arsenal. Some gifted athletes rely on their natural abilities and perform their best against tough competition or adversity by flipping on a switch. Nevertheless, it is difficult to be consistent in such performances. In short, athletes who think their natural ability is good enough to always win big in life will surely not be able to reach their full potential because they did not supply consistent effort to allow their minds to evolve. Consequently, to become an elite athlete, I knew I needed to have an unshakeable

CHAPTER 1: MINDSET

mindset.

Elite athletes constantly look to challenge themselves daily, without fail. While they have the talent and resources available, they still push themselves to improve their skills and attitude.

The power of the mind is extraordinary. It enables us to overcome most obstacles, regardless of how physically demanding they may seem. This was particularly exemplified in my first ironman, where I pushed through the physical exhaustion and fatigue to make it across the finish line with primarily the power of my mind. The physical aspect of our lives might seem to be the most important, but it is only a fraction of what truly matters.

Our mental aspect, on the other hand, should take precedence. This is because our thoughts and beliefs shape the way we make decisions and how we act. We can change our physical appearance or environment, but it is much harder to alter our mental state. It is often said that success is 80% mental and 20% physical. Although these percentages are arbitrary, they help cement the significant discrepancy between both variables.

Based on the above, we know that the most important part of any athlete's arsenal is how they cope and react to stimuli. Otherwise, we would be able to place any athlete in a vehicle and expect a similar outcome. For instance, "Ford vs. Ferrari." is one of my favorite movies that explain this phenomenon. Another solid case is the "Union Cycliste Internationale" (UCI) regulated bikes that are similarly all the same. Yet some cyclists stand out as 'superhuman' by finishing ahead of everyone by an enormous margin.

Even the athlete's recipe for training regimen is quite similar. Therefore, anyone could conclude that the only value that would make them set apart is their mindset. You could also learn to translate this attitude into other areas of your life. One of my favorites is knowing that I can reach further than anticipated. I did not even think I could finish the Epicdeca! All I knew was that I would not quit unless physically taken away from this challenge.

Additionally, it is easy to become overwhelmed and angry when treated unfairly, but the best course of action is to develop an attitude of growth in the face of mistreatment. With the right outlook, even difficult experiences can be used for growth and development.

Decision Making

Let us evaluate how to make an appropriate decision based on the circumstances. We all have moments where we think that we should have chosen differently. We make decisions at every instant of every day. Sometimes these choices are little and unimportant, and other times they profoundly impact our lives. In the end, the decisions you make and the actions you do are largely what governs how your day, your year, and your entire life turns out. If you understand what your needs are and if they are being met, you can gauge whether you are in a suitable position every time you render a decision.

Making the right choices in life can be daunting, and this is understandable, given the potential consequences of these decisions. The issue is that when faced with options, many people have a "deer in the headlights" flash. They end up not declaring a verdict at all because they are afraid of making the wrong choice. Almost all of us experience decision paralysis to some extent from time to time. It might be unsettling to realize the effects of your choices.

Making no decision, on the other hand, is a choice in and of itself, and it is usually always the wrong one. For instance, even if you make a mistake in choosing a crew, remember that you can always amend this choice in the future. But the idea is to make a choice, and at least you did formulate one. Additionally, it might severely harm your emotional stability, contentment, and self-assurance. When faced with the issue of choice paralysis, it is critical to understand that almost always, any verdict is going to be preferable to none.

You can begin taking charge of your life's consequences if you can get past the anxiety and uncertainty that are involved with making decisions. Providing quick judgments is one of the best methods to overcome decision paralysis. In fact, the capacity to act swiftly is a key factor in the triumph of many of the world's most successful entrepreneurs and leaders. Producing quick resolutions eliminates uncertainty, worry, and confusion. Instead of wasting time worrying about all the possibilities and trying to endlessly analyze every potential outcome, making a quick decision enables you to immediately begin devoting your efforts to following through on that option.

Generating prompt decisions will allow you to commit fully to your aspirations right away without allowing uncertainty and concern to slowly kill your choice over time. Thankfully, making quick decisions does not have to be challenging. Whatever choice you make, all you must decide is whether it is something you need or desire and whether it is worthwhile investing your time.

You will discover that conducting a selection is much simpler than you would have anticipated if you genuinely committed to it. Remember that once you have decided to do something, do not give up after the first obstacle you encounter.

CHAPTER 1: MINDSET

In the end, take responsibility for your decisions and learn from the process. If you have the right attitude and commit to your decisions, even mundane tasks can be rewarding. Doing something that you do not want to do is often a terrific way to motivate yourself and stay hungry for success. By taking the initiative, even if it is something small, you can start to build momentum.

Hire a Coach

Coaches have been around for centuries, even before professional organizations took hold. In ancient societies, guilds served as the training center and guidance for young minds, forming the foundation upon which expertise and knowledge would be built.

Today, however, we have seen a rise in charlatans who offer false promises and ineffective services. This has been the cause of a great deal of confusion and misunderstanding, leading many to disregard coaching altogether.

When it comes to hiring a coach, do not be afraid to take your time. Ask uncomfortable questions and get as much information from the candidate as possible before deciding. A coach should be someone who understands your goals and is passionate about helping you achieve them.

If you are not reaching the goals set for yourself,

it is important to take stock of what could be holding you back. It may be that you have set an unrealistic goal, or it could be that you are not taking consistent action toward your objective. At the same time, it could be that your coach is lacking in knowledge or skills in a particular area to reach the desired result.

A general rule of thumb is that if you have been with a coach for three months and have not seen any progress, then it is time to consider switching. Even if you believe in having found the right person, do not be afraid to make changes if you feel it is not the right fit. When I first started collaborating with a coach, I experienced a dip in my performance for the first few weeks.

By following the guidance of an experienced tutor, you can achieve success in any given field faster than on your own. This will allow you to make better decisions and ultimately reach the levels you aspire to. If you are looking for someone who can provide an honest and objective perspective, a coach could be the ideal solution.

An important key to success is recognizing that this mentor or a higher authority can be seen as a source of knowledge and guidance. As such, you should be able to respect the advice and trust their expertise. If you do not agree with something they say, you should feel comfortable asking questions to seek further clarification. This will help you to understand the perspective of your coach and allow you to make informed decisions about how to move forward. In the end, the decisions are yours. However, if the coach is experienced and knowledgeable in the field they are guiding you through, it is wise to trust them and follow their direction.

The journey toward self-actualization can be a difficult one, and by hiring a coach that is knowledgeable in the relevant area you seek, you can access their insight and expertise. This will help to keep you on track and ensure that you make the most of the opportunities presented to you.

What many fail to understand is that coaching is not just restricted to physical health and fitness. In fact, the knowledge and skills of a coach can be applied to all aspects of life, from mental health and development to career guidance and financial planning. Mentors can provide a wealth of wisdom that puts you on the path to your desired destination based on their relevant life experiences. Your attitude toward investing in yourself can make all the difference. If you want to see transformation and progress, be sure to invest in resources that will help you get there. For instance, when I wanted to race with top athletes, I invested in an elite triathlon coach.

Doing so allowed me to train with professional

athletes and acquire the strength to follow them. Even if your limiting beliefs tell you that you do not have the money or experience, it is vital to get your needs met. By investing in yourself, you are making capital spending on your future self. One that will enhance the quality of your life and often result in greater financial opportunities.

However, investing in yourself is not a one-time, quick-fix solution. It is about developing habits and routines that will support your long-term goals. Once you start to see the results, an investment in a coach may no longer seem like a hefty fee but rather a part of your planned expenditure.

My experience has taught me not to assume that just because someone is a fitness coach, they have the right skill set or experience to also help you with mindset and motivation. Similarly, a mentor that is great at helping you to become more motivated and focused may not be the ideal person to help you reach your physical fitness goals. Additionally, your partners or family members may be great to have around, but they might not necessarily be a coach and should not be expected to function as such. In some cases, it may be beneficial to seek out a coach rather than rely exclusively on your relatives for guidance.

This can be particularly true if you have experienced some trauma or are dealing with a difficult condition. They will also be able to provide an objective, unbiased perspective that your partner may not be able to offer. Additionally, the coach–client relationship is vastly different from that of a lover, providing an additional layer of support and healing.

Ultimately, do not settle for mediocrity; get the help you need to reach your peak performance. A great coach will not do the work for you but will enhance your resourcefulness so that you can find and apply the best solutions for yourself.

Strategize

Strategizing is more than simply making an initial plan. It requires deep consideration and thought, often with the input of experts or coaches, as opposed to the initial plan from decision-making, which only demands a commitment to a general outcome. There is often room to refine the strategy later when discussing it with your coach or councilors. It is important to pause and make sure that you are taking the time to craft a strategy that will work best for you rather than rushing through the process. Products and services may also be integral to the strategy process, such as selecting a bike for a triathlon. In the case of cycling gear selection, it is essential to research products or services that will give you the best outcome and to consider input from experts such as bike shops or other athletes. In comparison, the initial plan would only demand that you register for a triathlon.

Developing strategies is setting objectives and outlining schedules to accomplish your outcome. It is basically a step-by-step process where you will think and decide in detail about how to start and achieve a goal before beginning the work.

We design before starting something to ensure we reach the result and goals that we want, but it is also a measure of how far we have come or must go to reach that goal. Designing is essential as it allows us to stay focused on our goals despite changing situations. Additionally, a good strategy allows us to adapt depending on the situation but with the same outcome. Even if the plan changes tomorrow or until the beginning of the event, someone with a positive mindset will not have any trouble becoming flexible.

Value System

Your brain does not inherently know what is right and wrong; it needs to be taught. This is why it is important to take time for yourself to reflect and learn about the world around you. Acknowledging the boundaries of morality is a key part of deciding how to live your life, as it helps shape your decisions and enables you to act in alignment with your values.

You may be asking yourself how to navigate your

body through the maze of life. This can seem like an arduous task, but it is achievable with the right approach.

This two-question step process can help you develop a system of values and standards centered around healthy decision-making. When faced with a task or situation, ask yourself: Does this defy reality? Is this forcing someone else to commit a crime? If the answer is negative to both questions, you have all the information you need to make an informed decision. Any other additional questions or concerns should likely be answered along the way if you remain committed to your decision.

For your system of values and standards to have a positive impact on society, they must be grounded in doing good for humanity. If you are only focusing on the negative aspects of society, you may be perpetuating its downfalls.

Ultimately, it is up to you to decide what values and standards will guide your life. It takes time and effort to develop a set of rules that make sense to you, but by doing so, you can ensure that you are living by your values and creating a positive impact on the world around you.

However, if you find yourself feeling overwhelmed by this process, remember that it is okay to take things one step at a time. Start small and gradually build up until your system of values and standards becomes a natural part of your life.

Mind Games

Once I started cleaning up my thinking, I realized that some mental tricks could help me achieve more mental fortitude. When faced with tricky situations, it can be hard to know how to progress. It is easy to become overwhelmed or stuck in a rut. Fortunately, there are mental tricks that can help you out of these situations. These mental tricks can be used to reframe your thinking, break through a plateau, or create a whole new vision of success. They range from simple mindfulness exercises to more complex cognitive restructuring tools. The key is to find the ones that work for you and integrate them, individually or as a group set, into your daily routine.

Why — Uncovering your *why* can be a powerful way to unlock your full potential. When you understand the underlying motivations that drive you, it can provide clarity and direction in your life, allowing you to make meaningful progress toward achieving your goals. Your why can keep you grounded, provide a sense of purpose, and give you the strength to continue even when times get tough.

I can — The greatest impediment to success is often not a lack of ability or opportunity but the small voice in your head that says, "I can't." That voice is often a liar, and it can be silenced. You have the power to actively transform your "I can't" into "I can."

Present — The past is gone, and the present is here. You, like everyone, have made mistakes or done something wrong, but that does not mean you cannot learn from it and move forward. Reflection on what went wrong is important, but do not let it paralyze you from taking action in the present. Every experience is an opportunity for growth and learning. As long as you use the lessons of the past to inform your decisions in the present, you will be able to find success. Always remember that you have done the best with what you had at the time and strive to do even better going forward.

Gratefulness — Taking a moment each day to be mindful of what you are grateful for can have a monumental impact on your outlook and well-being. It can help you recognize the abundance of good things in your life while also teaching you to be grateful for even the smallest of blessings. Not only can it help you appreciate what you have, but it can also motivate and inspire you to strive for more. Gratitude also has the power to increase your self-esteem and a sense of purpose, boost your mental health, and even contribute to better relationships with others. Start the day by making a list of the things you are thankful for and post it somewhere that you can see daily.

Positivity — You have the power to take control of your life and fill it with positivity. When you take charge of your thoughts, you can drive yourself to greater heights. By focusing on the positives and keeping your mind open to innovative ideas, you can find yourself in the space of motivation and optimism. When you fill your mind with uplifting and inspiring ideas, it will create a spark within you and push you to be more than what you thought was possible. Take the time to reflect on what is positive in your life, and make sure you give yourself credit for all the hard work and effort you put in. It is important to take responsibility for keeping your life in balance. Focusing on the positive for this fleeting period does not mean you ignore the negative aspects of life. It means you are taking active steps to recognize the goodness in your life and deliberately choose to focus your attention there for this abbreviated period. This does not mean you will not eventually face your challenges or problems; it just means that you are consciously directing your attention to the aspects of life that bring joy in this specific moment.

Visualization — Picturing your future achievements and their outcome can help you to take control of your life in addition to attaining the future that you desire. When crafting your vision, make sure that you are clear and concise about your sought-after outcome.

Create a mental image of your future self already having achieved it, and use this to focus your energy and effort. Additionally, writing down a list of your goals can be incredibly helpful for staying on track as well as providing motivation and guidance along your journey.

Micro-goals — Breaking down your goals into smaller, more manageable chunks makes it easier to stay focused and motivated. By setting a series of micro goals, you create stepping stones, allowing you to build on each success and gain the necessary momentum required to reach your larger goal. Furthermore, having a series of smaller successes along the way will keep you feeling energized and remind you that you are on the right track.

The rule of 3 is a micro goal technique I use and recommend. Identify three daily activities that will bring you closer to your end goal. This may include reading related materials, studying a new skill, or simply taking time out of your day to reflect on what you have achieved and where you want to go.

Reward yourself — When it comes to motivating yourself to complete tasks, one potential solution is to reward yourself for a job well done. As with any external incentive, the reward should be meaningful to you. The idea is to make sure that the reward is proportional to the outcome. For example, if you put a lot of hard work and dedication into something, such as a major assignment, the reward should reflect that effort. On the other hand, completing a simpler task would likely warrant a smaller incentive.

That way, you can give yourself something to look forward to while also keeping your motivation and ambition in check. Additionally, to be proportionate to the task at hand, the reward should stay within your financial means and desires. Ultimately, the goal is to find a balance between expecting a reward and making sure that it does not become an unhealthy habit.

Chapter 2: Environment

"Anchor yourself where growth is present; otherwise, set sail."

~JD

Have you been struggling lately to stay motivated? Your current environment may have something to do with it. Occasionally, these negative impressions may come from a parent, lover, or close friend. Be ready to disconnect when the plug needs to be pulled, as you might be holding a cactus that only hurts you. It is not selfish to think of yourself. In fact, it is healthier to put your mask first before aiding someone on a plane if it is going through turbulence. You might be in a better condition to serve others from the same circle later. You could also view it as you are helping the person hurting you by moving away.

After all, our network helps us conquer our fears. With a strong community, we can also dictate who will have a more solid chance of survival. It is important to have a strong network or a like-minded community, as this may eventually determine your success in life. Throughout history, anyone who has achieved any noteworthy success has attributed it to having a circle of positive influence. The same can apply to us as well. Being part of a community with strong and like-minded people can be a huge motivating factor when it comes to achieving the things you want. Napoleon Hill is an author who popularized the concept of having a like-minded community. In his book, Think and Grow Rich, he refers to a community of like-minded individuals as a mastermind group. He defines the concept as;

CHAPTER 2: ENVIRONMENT

"Coordination of knowledge and effort, in a spirit of harmony between two or more people, for the attainment of a definite purpose."

So, why is it important to be connected to a like-minded community?

Support

It is so important to have people in our lives that we can rely on for support. That could mean offering advice and perspective or just being there to listen and lend an ear. Having someone who will support our decisions unconditionally is foolishness, as they would be neglecting their responsibility to provide guidance and counsel. The best kind of support comes when those we trust can offer constructive criticism and caution us about potential risks and things we may not have considered. This kind of support is invaluable, as it allows us to make informed decisions and to be aware of the potential consequences of our actions. It is through this kind of support that we can grow, learn, and continue making better decisions down the road.

Accountability

Having a system of accountability is essential for achieving success. It gives us the necessary push to break out of our comfort zone and expand our boundaries, pushing us to the next level. Taking ownership of our actions and being held accountable for the results is fundamental in this process.

Having like-minded peers in our corner is what will give us the support and motivation that we need to keep going. They will not listen to excuses but instead will encourage us to keep striving for the best possible outcome. Surrounding ourselves with peers who have similar goals and aspirations helps create an atmosphere of mutual support and accountability that is essential for success.

Cheering

Being part of a supportive and positive community can be a major catalyst behind success. As we share our successes with others, they will encourage us to reach for even higher levels of achievement. This, in turn, will boost our confidence and self-esteem, which will enable us to strive for more. We are capable of tremendous accomplishments when we are uplifted and cheered on by our peers and mentors. With a little guidance and support, we can accomplish more than we ever thought possible. So, remember to take advantage of the support from your community and use it as a powerful tool for achieving greatness.

Similar Language

Sports and triathlon communities have their

unique language that can be heard in conversations between members. Whether you are a seasoned athlete or just starting, learning the lingo will help you feel more connected to the group and make it easier to communicate with teammates. Here is a look at some of the main categories of words and phrases used in sports and triathlon communities.

Heartrate Monitor (HRM) — Your heart rate is an important indicator of your overall health and well-being. It can tell you a lot about how your body is functioning, how fit you are, and whether you need to take any measures to maintain a healthy lifestyle. A typical resting heart rate should be between 60-100 BPM or beats per minute. So, if your heart rate is higher or lower than this range, it is worth investigating the cause. For example, a consistently high heart rate could indicate that you are overtraining, while a persistently low heart rate could suggest an underlying health issue.

When it comes to tracking your heart rate, there are many options available. If you do not have any medical conditions or special needs for data accuracy, then a smartwatch is all you need. But if you do have specific needs or wish to have the most accurate data possible, then there are other devices like chest straps and wristbands that may be more suitable for you. Whatever device you choose, just make sure it can provide you with the data you need.

Blood pressure — Blood pressure is an important indicator of overall health and can be a warning sign of serious health issues. It is measured using two numbers, the systolic (top number) and diastolic (bottom number) blood pressure readings. The systolic reading measures the pressure in your arteries when your heart beats. The diastolic reading measures the pressure in your arteries when your heart rests between beats. During diastole, the heart muscle relaxes, and the chambers of the heart fill with blood, which causes a decrease in blood pressure. During systole, the heart contracts and pushes the blood out of the heart and into the large blood vessels of the circulatory system. This action increases blood pressure. In other words, blood pressure helps to show how much your heart is working to pump blood throughout your body.

Blood pressure is the amount of force that your blood exerts against the walls of your arteries. It is an important indicator of heart health and is used to measure how well the heart and circulatory systems are working. When participating in a sport, it can be useful to monitor your blood pressure as it indicates how hard you are pushing yourself physically. When engaging in physical activity, it is normal for your blood pressure to rise as the intensity of the sport increases. This allows your body to increase its oxygen and nutrient delivery to muscles and organs, which helps improve overall performance. However, it is important to ensure that your blood pressure does not exceed the normal range for an adult, which is around 120/80 mmHg.

VO2 max (Volume Oxygen Maximum) — VO2 max, also known as the maximum volume of oxygen uptake, is a measure of the maximum amount of oxygen that an individual can utilize during exercise. It is one of the most important indicators of aerobic fitness and reflects an individual's overall cardiorespiratory endurance. VO2 max can be measured using a variety of tests, such as running on a treadmill, cycling on a stationary bike, or exercising on an elliptical machine.

The higher the individual's VO2 max, the better their aerobic fitness level is and the more intense exercise they can manage. A person with a high VO2 max will be able to perform physical activities such as running or biking at higher speeds and for longer durations than an individual with a lower VO2 max. When you start to train to increase your VO2 max, remember that it will take some time and dedication. You should not expect a sudden boost in performance but a consistent effort over time that will yield tangible results.

Start by establishing a training plan and sticking to it. Make sure to include aerobic exercises as well as high-intensity interval training, which have been proven to be beneficial for increasing your VO2 max.

When you do these exercises, try to push yourself so that you are working close to your maximum capacity. Also, make sure to gradually increase the intensity of your workouts over time. In an ideal world, you would want to have both low blood pressure and a high VO2 max.

Altitude training is quickly gaining popularity in improving athletes' performance. By training at high altitudes, athletes can increase their VO2 max and improve their overall endurance. At higher altitudes, the air is thinner and contains less oxygen than at lower altitudes. This makes it more difficult for the body to perform strenuous activities, forcing it to work harder to meet oxygen demands and build stronger muscles. Training at altitude has been used by professional athletes and military personnel to increase their endurance and performance. By exercising in extreme conditions, you can challenge your body and push it further than what it is used to.

While altitude training is an effective workout to increase strength and improve performance, athletes need to be aware of the potential risks associated with it. Altitude training can put an extreme amount of strain on the body and mind, so it is important to be mindful of the mental stress it can cause. If done incorrectly, it could lead to an increase in depression and other mental health disorders. Therefore, it is important to be aware of the warning signs and get help from a mental health professional if needed.

Lactic acid — When your muscles become sore and fatigued after exercise, it is because of lactic acid. Lactic acid is produced during intense or prolonged physical activity and can cause that burning, heavy feeling in your muscles. It builds up faster than it can be metabolized, leading to the symptoms of exercise-induced muscle fatigue. While lactic acid can be uncomfortable, it is a normal part of the exercise process and helps to strengthen your muscles over time. Even though the feeling of lactic acid can be unpleasant at the moment, it is helping you get closer to reaching your fitness goals

Lactic acid is created when glucose goes through the metabolic process during exercise. It is a direct combination of lactate and hydrogen ions. However, recent research has challenged this notion, suggesting that these two entities may not be as intertwined as previously thought. Despite this debate, if one were present in the body without the other, it would be an incomplete and ineffective system.

Whether the hydrogen ion or the lactate is responsible for the fatigue, both need to be removed from the body. This process of removing lactic acid and its components is known as lactate clearance.

It is important to understand that lactic acid, which builds up in your muscles after exertive physical activity, can be cleared through a few simple steps. Essentially, the body needs time to rest, recover and flush out lactic acid that has built up during exercise. The production of lactic acid during strenuous exercise is, in a sense, the price you pay for physical exertion. It is a sign that you are working hard and pushing yourself to your limits. Lactic acid is the body's way of telling you that you have exceeded its capacity for natural energy production, and it needs to bring in an additional source of energy.

Power — The numbers that athletes measure themselves form a basis for comparison with oneself and with others. However, the key to success lies in striving to be better than one's previous self. By always striving to do better than before, you can keep improving your skills and performance at every stage of your athletic career. This attitude takes the focus away from competing with others and puts it firmly on oneself. If you decide to compare your numbers against previous results, as well as against others, you can get a sense of how good you are compared to the competition. Hopefully, you will use this to become the best you can be.

In sports, the margin of success is often razor-thin. That is why it is essential to understand that even if you finish only a few seconds behind a professional sprinter, you may be lightyears away from achieving his level of excellence. So, never get discouraged if you do not get the results, you want right away. Instead, work hard and keep trying. In time, you will reach your fullest potential.

Power meters have become increasingly popular for cyclists looking to track performance and measure their output. In cycling, power is measured in watts, which reflects the amount of force exerted on the pedals over a given period. A power meter can help cyclists accurately measure their power output and build their fitness, allowing them to optimize their training and performance.

Testing — Testing is an integral part of triathlon training and performance. It helps athletes understand how their bodies are responding to the demands of the sport and provide valuable data and feedback to inform training decisions. Testing can be done in a variety of ways, from simple time trials to more sophisticated laboratory testing.

It is also worth noting that you will not be able to replicate exactly what you do in a training session, as certain factors cannot be controlled. It all depends on many aspects, such as weather conditions, terrain, the adrenaline of a race, and even your mental state during the race.

However, that does not mean that you cannot prepare for the race by running tests. I included some of the most important ones below for each discipline of triathlon. Then, you can use these basic equations to calculate approximately what your time would be in a triathlon event based on these tests.

The Critical Swim Speed (CSS) test is the most popular testing system used by coaches to track and measure their athletes' swimming performance. As described by Wakayoshi, the CSS test requires a 400-meter and 200-meter swim at maximum speed with a fully recovered rest period in between. For those looking to determine their CSS, an online calculator can be used or the difference between both groups can be divided to get your result. Understanding and keeping track of your CSS is essential for any swimmer looking to progress their performance in the pool. Through monitoring of your CSS, coaches can adjust training regimes accordingly and ensure that athletes are performing at peak levels.

In cycling, the FTP test, or Functional Threshold Power test, is a measure of your potential power output. It consists of cycling for 20 minutes at the highest intensity you can sustain with the aim of generating as much power as you can. Once you have completed the test, the average watts produced in those 20 minutes minus 5% will be your functional threshold power. Additionally, a good warm-up before a 20-minute FTP test is essential. It should include one or two vigorous efforts of four to five minutes each. This is important because it helps you prepare mentally and physically for the test, allowing your body to adjust to the increased intensity.

The FTP test is one of the most important metrics to measure in cycling. It is important to track this number as it gives cyclists an understanding of other cycling numbers such as watts per kilogram, critical power, and watts per minute. In the world of competitive sports, watts per kilogram is a valuable metric for athletes and coaches to compare riders with different body compositions objectively, as well as gauge how effective an athlete's training is in preparation for a certain event.

Running is a skill that requires an understanding of speed and distance. Measuring your running performance can be done in terms of minutes per kilometer or miles. The use of min/km instead of km/min is an important way to measure your running performance. While speed may vary over time, a pace reflects a steady and consistent rate over a certain distance.

The equation created by Pete Riegel is an invaluable instrument for any runner looking to increase their performance. As a research engineer and marathoner, Riegel was in a unique position to combine his experience with data-driven insights to develop this formula.

By using the T2 = T1*(D2/D1) ^1.06 equation, runners can predict their performance for a variety of distances. As an example, if you knew it took 20 min to run 5 km, the formula can predict how long it will take you to run a marathon of 42.2 km. Simply plug in the numbers: T2 = 20*(42.2/5) ^1.06. A small decay of 1.06 to the power of this universal ratio is an equation that takes our body and mental fatigue into account. When using a combination of sports, such as in triathlon or increasing the distance significantly, we could increase this final generalized number higher. Despite the inherent imperfection of this equation, it remains a useful tool for acquiring an overall understanding of how long our competition may take. Even so, if we wish to refine our estimates, mathematical modeling should be employed.

Threshold — Athletic success is not just about hitting a certain level of power and speed. It requires an understanding of your threshold and the ability to push yourself beyond it. When you understand where your threshold lies, you can set goals and work toward reaching them. This will help you increase your capabilities and reach the highest level of performance possible. Developing a sense of your thresholds is an important part of any athlete's journey, and it should be seen as a challenge to push yourself further. With dedication and hard work, you can go beyond your current threshold and reach new heights in your athletic endeavors.

Community Expectations

Failure — There is no escaping the fact that people will fail you in life. You can change your expectations and accept this as part of life, or you can continue to be disappointed. The choice is yours. The ability to change expectations is an invaluable skill, as it allows you to focus on the positives and accept that life can be unpredictable. You should not be completely accepting of every failure. Set reasonable expectations and take appropriate actions to address issues that arise.

Failure is a part of life, and it is quite easy to allow our missteps to lead to feeling defeated. But what separates those who succeed from those who do not is their willingness to accept failure and move on. Instead of getting stuck in a cycle of disappointment and discouragement that leads to stagnation, those who persevere can recognize the underlying cause of failure and use it as an opportunity for growth. As a result, they can reassess their goals and find new paths to success. Failing is not something to be ashamed of; it is a part of life and a chance to learn and grow. In this world of improbabilities, having the tougher skin and resilience to keep going is essential for anyone who wants to move forward and reach their goals. Do not let failure define you; use it as a stepping stone to greater things. Be ready to accept failure, learn from it, and then make the changes you need to move on and succeed.

People Change — When it comes to making a change in the community, there are two paths one can take. The first is hitting rock bottom and coming to understand that the current situation is not sustainable. Making a change out of necessity can be difficult and scary, but it can also bring about an appreciation for the opportunities presented by change. The second path is the observation of change. Looking around and noticing what works for others can provide inspiration and motivation to make changes in one's life. Seeing how others have had an influence on their lives can be the spark that inspires one to make changes to their own lives. The only thing you can truly control is yourself. Your ability to make changes in your life lies within your capacity to be responsible for how you think, feel, and act. You must be willing to take ownership of your life and commit to making the necessary changes for yourself. This is not a task to undertake lightly, as it requires significant effort to make lasting change. It is only when you have reached despair or consciously taken action to alter your path that you can begin to make progress. If you want to notice any changes within your group, then you need to be willing to take the first step and lead by example. To make a difference, you must start with yourself.

Fears — Fears are a natural part of life, and we should never be ashamed to admit them. Unfortunately, some people take advantage of our fears to manipulate and control us. Hence why we must be wary of this and always strive to confront these fears rather than cowering in the face of them. By facing our fears head-on, we can begin to understand and even overcome them, allowing us to take back control of our emotions and reactions. As a result, we can gain greater handling of our lives and the direction we want to take them.

We must remember that everyone has their way of dealing with fear. Some might prefer to talk it out, while others may choose to go for a run or start a new hobby. The trick is to recognize these fears and embrace them rather than run away from them. As I have come to learn, there are many opportunities for growth, even in the midst of difficulty. In fact, this is where true transformation often originates from. I have come to understand that when we face and accept our fears, we can move beyond them and find strength in ourselves.

We can use these experiences to propel us forward and motivate us to become better versions of ourselves. We can take whatever laughter or ridicule we receive and use it as fuel to make our dreams a reality. We can also recognize that our fears are often nothing more than illusory and keep them in perspective. With this approach, we can act with confidence and courage as we move forward in our lives.

Understand people — The priority here is to surround yourself with people who have similar goals and values as you. That way, they will be able to help push and inspire you to reach your objectives. However, it is also important to stay open-minded and acknowledge the different opinions that are present in any given situation. This does not mean you have to agree with them, but it does mean that you should be willing to consider and even embrace new perspectives. By being open to different points of view, you can learn from other people's experiences and gain insight into topics that may have been overlooked.

It is also important to recognize and accept your strengths and weaknesses. It is unrealistic to think that you are better than everyone in all aspects of life, and no one should expect that from you. Instead, it is important to understand what your strengths are and use them to your advantage to benefit the lives of others. This does not mean ignoring areas of improvement, but that you should focus on what you do well and use those skills to help those around you.

By creating an environment that is conducive to growth and success, you will be able to build a dedicated support system that will help you achieve your goals. So do not be afraid to reach out and make connections.

Chapter 3: Escapism

"A lack of decision is a decision."

~JD

When life gets too overwhelming, we need to take a step back from reality. In fact, it is recommended and an effective way of experiencing a few moments of respite when life's hardships seem to bring us down.

In a lot of ways, escapism is healthy and helpful. It offers many advantages to weary individuals close to burnout. Escapism helps reduce stress, prevent a breakdown, and increases our feelings of determination. Doing so by recharging our psychological strength is an integral component of building a stronger sense of self-pleasure. The process of revitalization rises rapidly when we know how to please ourselves consciously.

There are many ways by which people can escape from the challenges of life, at least for a little while. We take refuge in television, books, daydreaming, cooking, working out, social media platforms, meditation, and even sports. These are all great ways to take a step back from life for a few moments. When it comes to which coping mechanism everyone should use, there is no single right answer. We all have different desires and experiences, so the best approach is to make decisions that are in line with our values and preferences. Everyone deserves to experience some sort of escape from life when it gets too consuming. When life becomes overwhelming, it is important to take a step back and ask yourself what is working and what is not. Taking a break from everyday life can give you a chance to re-evaluate your goals, reset your perspective, and get back on track with new enthusiasm. The major difference between unhealthy and healthy is the length of time at which someone partakes in said behaviors. Escapism becomes damaging when we take it too far into the realm of avoidance. In this case, we begin to ignore and avoid our responsibilities. These actions eventually become unhealthy coping mechanisms for dealing with life. Escapism must ideally be used as a tool to refuel us rather than avoid life and its stressors that we need to address eventually.

To do so, it is essential to look at the basic anatomy of the body and how it works to understand how to cope with stress, worries, and other challenges in life. Our body is made up of a series of systems that work together to maintain the balance and functioning of our physique. For instance, by understanding the delicate balance of the endocrine and nervous systems, we may be able to identify the symptoms of some common illnesses in our life. For example, endocrine fatigue is a condition caused by an imbalance of hormones that may lead to fatigue, chronic stress, and even depression.

Endocrine and Nervous system

The endocrine system is responsible for producing

hormones that regulate your bodily functions, so when we say, "it's probably just your hormones," it means that our body is producing hormones that are affecting our mood. However, this process is so much more complicated than a simple statement. The endocrine system works in tandem with the nervous system to keep our bodies in balance and help us respond to different stimuli. For example, when we are angry or stressed, our adrenal glands secrete hormones that can increase our heart rate and make us more alert.

Understanding how the endocrine system works can help us learn to better control our hormones and utilize them to our advantage. For instance, when an athlete is preparing to compete in a race, understanding how their body works can help them increase the production of certain hormones that can give them the edge they need to perform well. Learning about the endocrine and central nervous system (CNS) can also help us understand our bodies better so we can figure out how to best prepare for a race.

Nervous System

The nervous system is an incredible and powerful piece of machinery that serves as the ultimate communication system between the brain and the body. It allows us to interact with our environment, reason, and make decisions. The brain is the control center for the nervous system. It processes sensory information from the body, helps to regulate and coordinate movement, and produces thoughts and emotions. The spinal cord is the conduit through which all signals from the brain to the body and vice versa travel. The complex network of nerves throughout the body carries messages from the brain to and from all organs, muscles, and other parts of the body. Our nervous system is a remarkable structure that allows us to process information, think logically, understand our environment, and respond to it.

CNS and Endocrine Distinction

The nervous and endocrine systems both play particularly important roles in maintaining your body's health, but they do so in vastly separate ways. The nervous system acts like a rapid-response network, sending signaling molecules called neurotransmitters quickly to trigger reactions in an emergency. On the other hand, the endocrine system is slower and more subdued. This system works to help your body adjust to long-term changes in your environment and aids in growth, development, and metabolism. It is an important system that provides the body with the resources it needs to endure the ever-shifting environment we live in. Put simply, the nervous system is an active system, while the endocrine system provides long-term effects. Both systems are integral to a healthy body, and they work together to help you reach your highest levels of physical and mental function.

Endocrine System

The endocrine system is an essential part of the human body. Its glands secrete hormones that regulate how our bodies function and respond to distinct kinds of stimuli. The major glands participating in the endocrine system include the thyroid and parathyroids, adrenals, gonads (ovaries or testes), thymus, pancreas, pineal, pituitary, and hypothalamus.

Each gland has its specific function. For instance, the thyroid gland is responsible for producing hormones that regulate our body's metabolism, while the parathyroid glands are responsible for maintaining our body's calcium balance.

The adrenal glands are just as important. Located on top of each kidney, these little hat-shaped organs are responsible for releasing hormones like corticosteroids and epinephrine that help regulate our blood pressure and metabolism.

The reproductive organs are also crucial components of the endocrine system. In humans, these organs are usually either ovaries or testes. The ovaries are located on either side of the uterus, where they produce estrogen and progesterone. Testes, on the other hand, are located in a pouch outside the body and are responsible for producing testosterone and sperm. Each of these organs has an incredibly vital role to play in reproduction, and they are essential components of the endocrine system.

The thymus is a small gland located in the upper part of the chest and is responsible for producing white blood cells that help fight infections and destroy abnormal cells. It is largely responsible for the development of our immune system and plays a critical role in keeping us healthy.

The pancreas is a key player in the endocrine system. This organ is located behind the stomach, and it produces two hormones: insulin and glucagon. Insulin helps regulate the amount of sugar in our bloodstream, while glucagon works to break down stored sugar for energy. Together, these hormones help keep our blood sugar in balance and ensure that our cells have the energy they need to function properly.

The pineal gland, pituitary gland, and hypothalamus, located in the head, form the core of this system, controlling our hormones and regulating bodily processes. Furthermore, the pineal body is located in the middle of the brain. It produces the hormone melatonin, which helps our body know when it is time to sleep. Melatonin is also involved in regulating other hormones, and its production can be affected by luminosity or stress.

The pituitary gland is located below the brain; it is usually no larger than a pea. But it plays a key role in controlling many functions of the other endocrine glands. It produces hormones like growth hormone, which is involved in growth and development, and thyroid stimulating hormone, which helps regulate the production of hormones by the thyroid gland.

Finally, the hypothalamus, located at the base of the brain, is an incredible organ that acts as a bridge between the nervous and endocrine systems. It is the source of emotional and physical regulation, performing many distinct functions within the body. It secretes hormones that stimulate the release of other hormones from the pituitary gland, and it also helps to regulate our sleep, temperature, appetite, and blood pressure. By coordinating this intricate web of hormones, the hypothalamus helps to keep our bodies running smoothly and efficiently.

Hormones

Glands act kind of as a bridge between the brain and the body, allowing hormones to be released into the bloodstream. These hormones are then pumped back into the system through the bloodstream, searching for specific receptors on cells that can recognize their signals. When a hormone binds to its receptor, it causes changes in the cell, often by increasing or decreasing the activity of certain processes. This progression can affect millions of cells throughout the body, creating a multitude of changes that allow us to adapt as necessary. It is an incredibly complex system and one that should be respected for its power and potential. Learning about the intricate world of hormones will help unlock new levels of understanding in ourselves, enabling us to make better lifestyle choices and stay ahead of any potential problems.

Most hormones are composed of either amino acids or steroids. When the levels of these hormones in the body become too low (hypo) or too high (hyper), it can lead to a disruption of the body's equilibrium which is also called homeostasis. It is well-established that hormones have a significant impact on our moods. Changes in hormone levels can influence the production of certain chemicals in the brain, which in turn can affect our emotional state. But it is not just hormones that are responsible for our moods. Neurotransmitters and social factors also play a part. So, when it comes to managing your emotions, it is important to understand the body's regulatory system and how unhealthy habits can disrupt hormonal balance and cause emotional distress. Taking steps to maintain healthy hormone levels is essential for maintaining emotional well-being. By doing this, we can ensure that our endocrine system functions as intended and create an environment where we can best manage our emotional states.

Hormone Cascades

The hormone cascade phenomenon describes a chain reaction of hormones that can take some time to settle down. The time it takes for each system to act is vastly different. Neurotransmitters work within milliseconds, whereas hormones take minutes to days. This reflects the complexity of their respective tasks.

A prime example of a hormonal cascade is the hypothalamic-pituitary-adrenal axis or HPA-Axis. This complex interaction between three glands is responsible for regulating many of our body's functions, such as helping us manage stress and aiding digestion. This phenomenon is inextricably linked to our nervous system, as it plays a key role in the fight-or-flight response.

Common Hormones and Neurotransmitters

Neurotransmitters and hormones are essential for the functioning of all living organisms, including humans. They help regulate body processes such as growth, development, reproduction, and mood. Neurotransmitters are proteins that allow for the sending of signals from one neuron to another. Hormones, on the other hand, can be either proteins, lipids, or cholesterol-based molecules and are released into the bloodstream, where they affect distant parts of the body. When you think about the neurotransmitters and hormones that can have a major influence on your life, some that stand out.

These include serotonin, dopamine, endorphin, oxytocin, adrenaline, cortisol, and testosterone. Serotonin is the "feel-good" neurotransmitter that helps us feel calm and relaxed. Dopamine is the reward-seeking neurotransmitter that motivates us to act and get things done. Endorphin is also called the runner high because it creates a sense of euphoria. Oxytocin is the "love hormone" responsible for social connection, trust, and bonding. Adrenaline can give you a surge of energy, strength, and alertness when your body needs it most. Cortisol is known as the "stress hormone" because it prepares your body for fight or flight in times of danger or distress. And lastly, testosterone is a powerful masculine hormone that drives men's libido, muscle mass, aggression, and competitiveness. Each of these hormones plays a key role in our body, and being able to collaborate with them in balance can have tremendous effects on our physical and mental health. Of course, it is always best to work with a professional when dealing with any of these hormones, as there is a delicate balance that needs to be maintained. The good news is, with the right guidance and understanding, we can learn to work with these hormones and neurotransmitters and create a healthier, more balanced life.

Body Reactions

Our bodies are designed to survive and protect us from any potential danger, whether it be physical or psychological. But although our bodies can recognize potential threats and react accordingly, we cannot rely on them to make decisions for us. It is up to us to take control of our brains and be conscious of our decisions. We must understand that our brains are fallible and will sometimes lead us astray. With the right guidance, however, we can learn to control our emotions and make conscious decisions that are in our best interests.

We can learn to recognize potential triggers and how to confront them in order to stay on the right path. We can also learn to fake certain emotions in order to secrete the right ones at the right time, thereby avoiding unhealthy habits and situations that could harm us.

When it comes to performing in a race, our bodies respond in astonishing ways. We may not be aware of the physiological processes that occur while we are in the midst of a race, but they are happening, nonetheless. The following is a perfect world scenario where anyone would be able to take advantage of those processes and use them to their benefit.

For comprehension and reinforcement of the concept of hormones and their application, an example has been developed. The example starts with the simple act of competing in a triathlon, which would cause us to secrete testosterone. This hormone provides us the courage and resilience to take on a risk-filled challenge, be it in a sport like a triathlon or in life. The fear of failure in a triathlon can be crippling, and so adrenaline would flood our system to face the unknown. However, you could tap into your serotonin reserves by eating something that will activate your digestive system and calm down your anxiety.

The sense of risk-taker quickly leaves as you spend time together with friends and receive a healthy dose of oxytocin. After waving goodbye to your friends, you choose to get a dopamine rush by entering chilly water or performing pushups. Not only will you receive a burst of dopamine, but also an instant rush of accomplishment and self-confidence. Cortisol has been secreted throughout your event as various levels of stress have been applied throughout the competition. Finally, when you start crossing the finish line of a triathlon event, your body releases endorphins.

This natural high is a reward for getting through the event, and it serves as an encouragement for the next time. It is also worth mentioning that this illustration was constructed on the assumption that I am only referring to the chief secreted hormones, not the consecutive stages.

The cycle of increase and decrease of stress hormones and their consequential effect on our performance is something to embrace rather than shy away from. It is an elegant and powerful tool if used correctly. To use the cycle to its fullest potential, you must understand that you cannot remain at peak performance for too long. Doing so could lead to a shock to the system with potentially devastating consequences. Learning how to use the power of this cycle can give you the edge that could make all the difference in any training session or race.

Hormones are our body's way of signaling us to act. In a dangerous situation, the body will often secrete adrenaline as a signal for us to act. It is the primary hormone secreted in that instance, and it serves as a warning for us to fight, flee, or be shy. However, other hormones, such as cortisol, will also be secreted. It is important to note that all these hormones work together in a complex system to help us respond to different stimuli. By understanding the main secreted hormones and how they interact, we can better understand our psychological responses to situations. This insight will help us to make informed decisions and better manage our emotions.

Not only are these theories utilized in athletics, but they may also be employed in overcoming addiction. For example, cravings for alcohol can be a symptom of an underlying need for connection and belonging. If you find yourself wanting to drink only because it makes you feel connected and accepted, it might be time to explore other ways of getting these emotions in your life. Finding activities that generate oxytocin can be a wonderful way to make connections with others without the need for alcohol. This might include joining clubs or volunteering, engaging in meaningful conversations with friends and family, or simply taking the time to appreciate your relationships. While drinking alcohol and conversing with friends can be enjoyable in moderation, it is important to remember that when our bodies crave it too much, it can be a sign that something else is missing in our lives. Taking the time to explore healthier and more meaningful activities can help to fill this void and make us feel connected without the need for alcohol.

It is important to understand that the body does not respond quickly when it comes to hormones. The slow changes they create can cause lasting transformation, but it is a process that requires patience. Lasting change does not happen overnight,

so do not despair if you have not seen the results, you want just yet. Keep trusting in your body's process, and you will see the transformation begin to take shape.

For example, certain drugs can increase the secretion rate of certain hormones in unhealthy doses. While this might lead to an increase in pleasurable feelings, it can also cause a host of physical and emotional problems when a person decides to return to healthy hormonal sources. This is why it is essential to understand the role hormones play and how they can be managed healthily. Doing so can help us better navigate life's challenges and make sure we are taking care of ourselves both mentally and physically.

When it comes to drugs and alcohol, the same concept applies to actions such as watching pornography. By ingesting an unhealthy amount of pornographic content, we subject our brains to overly elevated levels of dopamine while decreasing our levels of testosterone unnaturally. This has the effect of creating unrealistic expectations for real-life relationships, as it is impossible for them to compete with the dopamine rush created by pornographic content. As a result, we can become addicted to pornography, and our libido can become so desensitized that it fails to respond to real-life relationships.

CHAPTER 3: ESCAPISM

Therefore, creating a vicious circle of addiction and producing dire consequences by disrupting your testosterone and oxytocin levels. Without these hormones, you would find yourself unable to desire competition or form meaningful connections with others. This can lead to isolation, low self-confidence, and overall dissatisfaction with your life. Thus, it is important to keep your testosterone and oxytocin levels balanced to stay competitive, connected, and have a general sense of contentment.

With all the notions we have of the neuro-endocrine system, it is now easy to explain that if a person has been in excess or in demand of a certain hormone for an extended period, that person would need to fill that void somehow. There are multiple ways to do so in a healthy way. However, they do not provide as much of a spike as a chemically induced drug or unrealistic expectations of reality as in the case of pornography. Essentially any type of way that distorts reality opens the door to addiction. In my opinion, an addiction is anything that takes you away from your responsibilities.

Even something like an Ultraman or an Ironman could be viewed as someone who is escaping. It always comes down to the individual's needs and chemical demands. It may be helping couples to read that their partner who has low dopamine levels because of his pornographic use may need to go to the extreme of an Ironman to reach a similar high in dopamine in a healthier form.

Although this may not seem healthy for a normal onlooker, you only need to know that, unless you have a preexisting medical condition, the human body is always looking for homeostasis.

It is important to remember that regaining control over your biology and your brain is a process that can take years. It may even depend on the individual and their specific needs. The key is to identify what hormone drives the symptoms and then find a way to release that hormone in its natural form.

That way, the body can slowly restore homeostasis in its time and find balance. This is a long-term commitment that will have to be kept in order to see the desired outcome. Allow yourself the time for change and be open to trying new things that can help you achieve balance.

Good Escapism

Distractions, when used in moderation, can be healthy and beneficial for our mental well-being. It can be anything from taking a week off work to going on an adventure, spending time with friends, or simply taking a few minutes to be in the moment. Allowing ourselves a brief pause from everyday stressors can allow us to focus on something else and gain a better understanding of the direction of our lives.

When we introduce these in our life, we feel re-energized and replenished to take over the day and all it brings. Diversions should always be momentary and brief, as it invigorates us to return to reality soon after a short interruption.

After a well-deserved temporary halt, we can face our challenges with renewed strength and a fresh mind. We might possibly even have a completely transformed outlook.

Remarkable changes cannot be expected overnight. Patience and persistence are vital elements to achieving any goal. Give yourself time for the recent changes to occur and become a permanent aspect of your life.

It usually takes a minimum of three tries in the right direction before you can notice the benefits, and a habit can take up to six weeks to become part of your routine. You must give yourself time to adjust to the unfamiliar environment and changes around you.

Bad Escapism

On the other hand, we use avoidance and engage in distractions to run away from our problems. Unhealthy escapism is used to ignore glaring issues consciously or unconsciously for an extended period. We harm ourselves terribly by avoiding our problems and engaging in unhealthy coping mechanisms. Doing this can hurt our responsibilities and our relationships.

Over time, our underlying problems will remain unaddressed and detrimental to our growth. Dodging reality should always remain momentary, and we should use healthy coping mechanisms to find relief. However, daydreaming can slowly become a damaging way of life with unhealthy choices. Moreover, coping mechanisms may be detrimental or beneficial contingent on the circumstance and how they are managed by your body. For example, a vacation may revitalize your body or drain your energy depending on your needs and choices.

While people have their reasons for choosing avoidance and unhealthy coping mechanisms, I am here to tell you to choose better for yourself. Even when the world seems dark and bleak, you need to learn how to embrace your helplessness and turn it into acceptance and strength.

For instance, a person who drinks too much alcohol and hurts others may choose to avoid such behaviors for a while. Then they may choose to return to it later at a moderate pace once they have achieved a prolonged period of sobriety and feel more in control.

CHAPTER 3: ESCAPISM

Loneliness

Solitude is healthy, and everyone should experience it at some point to a certain degree. No matter how difficult it may feel, if you are being mistreated or consistently treated with disrespect, then loneliness might be the better option. It can be hard to make this decision, but you must remember that you cannot put a price on self-respect. Nevertheless, loneliness can have a damaging impact, and from my experience, the greatest challenge I encountered was being alone.

Moreover, most of the top elite soldiers in the world agree that the nastiest torture practice anyone can endure is extended periods of isolation. Additionally, a person may feel these emotions of emptiness amidst being surrounded by a multitude of individuals or having millions of followers. This might be due to the desire for tangible connections. Nonetheless, loneliness does not have to be a negative emotion. In fact, it can be an opportunity for growth and exploration. Loneliness can be a catalyst for change, as it allows us to confront our fears and doubts and come out stronger than ever before. It is also a time to reflect on our lives and the choices we make. We must find the courage within ourselves to take ownership of our lives and make tough decisions when needed. Despite wanting someone to constantly tell us what to do, it is not always possible, and thus, we must develop the mental fortitude to make decisions on our own. Being alone allows for an honest assessment of your future and knowing if you are devoting your time wisely. When it comes to utilizing your time wisely, the 90/10 rule is a great guideline. 90% of your energy should be focused on what you are already gifted in, and the remaining 10% should be devoted to improving on skills that need development. Investing in yourself through self-reflection can be incredibly beneficial, particularly when you are alone.

Forgiveness

Forgiveness is often attached to, in my opinion, an erroneous definition which is to forget all wrongdoings. Moreover, some people often told me that forgiving means never bringing up the incident ever again. This way of thinking brings about a loss of their history. It is important to remember that one should never forget the wrongdoings of others; we must learn from our mistakes and the ones of others. By remembering the wrongdoings, we do not give in to foolish behavior. As Albert Einstein said, "The definition of insanity is doing the same thing over and over again and expecting different results." So, forgive those who have wronged you, but do not forget the lessons that you have learned from it.

CHAPTER 3: ESCAPISM

From my viewpoint, forgiveness is a type of mercy to be able to reason about an incident with the objective of transforming the negative element of anger in your system into a constructive pathway. The anger should still be present in your system. Although, in this case, the emotion would propel you forward. This form of compassion can be a powerful tool to change your life. Can you imagine the energy you are wasting holding on to all those grudges? For my part, I chose to understand my pain and use it as a catalyst to generate a constructive life that would eventually help others.

I also kept in mind that you cannot control how people treat you. People may put you down and project their fears unto you. They only win if you do not forgive, then you eventually end up hurting yourself. You can let them get to you or have a hunger mentality. A hunger mindset in this context is when you wish you had a stronger bond between all your connections despite offenses. People will make mistakes around you, and they might even fail to meet your expectations. The goal is to forgive and set the bar of your hopes at a reasonable height. When a person does not meet this standard, be kind enough to move on. This can also necessitate that you explain to the person that they have not met your targeted objective.

Technology

The way we communicate has evolved exponentially over the last few years. The telephone and the internet might be some of the best inventions of all time. Despite that, as we grow exponentially in technology, we also decrease proportionally in terms of connections. Consequently, I stayed away from social media during the event. It is essential to regulate the stimuli we get from our phones and social media so we avoid overdosing or being subjected to unhealthy electromagnetic waves.

You could also ensure that these waves are not constantly in sensitive areas. A wise option is the use of a Bluetooth headset instead of putting the phone constantly on your ear or near your face. Regardless, you must ensure you can disconnect from any screen regularly to stay linked to reality. In the event you are unable to disconnect completely for an extended period, you may wish to allocate a certain percentage of your time spent watching screens to be away from any device. You might not view it as a meaningful change, yet over time, it could become substantial.

Chapter 4: Fuel Body & Mind

"What you allow into your mind is the key to creating a life that is worthy of your potential."

~JD

According to the first law of thermodynamics, whatever energy you bring into a system must eventually be used or become waste. This applies in many areas of life, not just physics and engineering. In the same way that we cannot keep adding energy to a closed system without consequence, we also cannot keep putting something into our lives without getting something out of it. That does not necessarily mean that it must be wasted. You can choose to make effective use of what goes in and direct the energy where you want it to go.

To be able to push my body and mind to their limits, I had to learn how to maximize my workouts. This is why I believe it is vital to treat your body like a temple. Fuel it in the same way professional athletes do so that you can boost your energy levels and improve your performance during exercise. When treating our bodies with the respect that they deserve, we can tap into a seemingly unlimited reserve of energy to power us through our workouts.

By properly fueling yourself, you will be able to get the most out of your training regardless of the environment you are in.

But first, let us discuss the anatomy and how the body interacts with its environment at a straightforward level. This should provide you enough information to make basic decisions toward your research to discover your ultimate peak performance. The main categories of biological macromolecules are carbohydrates, lipids, proteins, and nucleic acid. Additionally, electrolytes are critical for satisfactory cellular efficiency.

Electrolytes

Sodium is in a category of its own and is essential for our bodies to function as they should. Like potassium, calcium, and magnesium, it helps to regulate fluid balance, nerve conduction, and muscle contraction. Proper hydration requires more than just water. It also needs an adequate supply of sodium. Without enough of this key electrolyte, our cells will not be able to absorb and utilize the necessary amounts of water. Sodium plays an essential role in our bodies, helping to keep the electric signals that run through us firing on all cylinders.

Without sodium, those signals would be weaker and more erratic, leading to muscle cramps, irregular heartbeats, and disruption of skeletal functions. As you may already be aware, our cells and organs rely on fluids to maintain their structure and function. If we do not drink enough water, our bodies become dehydrated, which can lead to a range of issues, including fatigue, headaches, and difficulty concentrating. Sweating during exercise is a normal process that may be altered when you exert yourself to the max. During intense levels of activity, dehydration can be life-threatening.

To avoid becoming dehydrated to the point where you are risking your health for a competition that may only last a few hours, pay attention to your sweat rate, the environment you compete in, and the quality of products that you ingest. It is difficult to say how much liquid and sodium mixture is necessary because people have various sweat rates, and the conditions of the sports are diverse.

I discovered a formula after doing multiple testing with a company called Precision Fuel and Hydration. This company constructs personalized plans to fuel athletes' workouts, and as the name suggests, they specialize in hydration. The best way to determine any person's basic sweat rate is to monitor body weight fluctuations before and after exercise without drinking any fluid.

The total weight loss is then calculated and registered as the total amount of fluid loss. This number can be viewed as the replenishment requirement. Urine coloration is one way to verify your level of hydration. If it is clear or light yellow, it is a sign that you are well-hydrated. On the other hand, if your urine is darker in color, it may mean that you need to drink more liquid. According to the American College of Sports Medicine, athletes should start drinking fluids at least four hours before their workout. This will reduce the need to guzzle water while exercising, which can also upset the stomach. There are diverse options available when choosing which fluid to drink. Sports drinks usually have ingredients such as fast-acting sugars and electrolytes like sodium and potassium. However, simply drinking water is just as fine if you are doing moderately leveled exercise. Keep a look at salt on the skin and clothes after a workout. If the sweat rate is high or you are experiencing cramping, it might be best to drink a beverage with sodium.

One reason I used Precision Fuel and Hydration is that, unlike other companies, their products are simply broken down into two separate categories — sugar and salt. This also makes math much easier when it comes to calculating my intake requirements in the middle of a race when I have not been following the original plan.

Carbohydrates

The term "carbohydrate" is a misnomer. It was erroneously created to indicate that these cells mainly provide hydration. It was only later discovered that they are an energy source. A better name for them would be "glucid" or simply "carbs." Regardless of the term we use, these cells still play a vital role in providing fuel for our bodies and should not be overlooked when optimizing nutrition. The importance of carbohydrates cannot be overstated. Without them, our bodies will not have the energy they need to go about their daily activities.

Though simple carbohydrates or "simple sugars" are an easy source of energy for the body to use right away, they do not provide lasting energy like complex carbohydrates do. Complex carbohydrates are broken down more slowly and provide the body with a steady source of energy over a longer period, making them an important part of any healthy diet. So, while simple sugars can be enjoyed in moderation, complex carbohydrates should make up the bulk of your daily carbohydrate intake. This statement is also based on the level and type of activity

Glucose is a major component in most sugary foods, such as syrup, sports drinks, and desserts. Its capacity to bypass the liver and head directly to the skeletal muscle system may explain why many people complain of joint pain and fatigue after eating a meal with elevated levels of simple sugar.

The upside of eating glucose is by having a fast filtration rate, glucose can be ingested during a race or workout and improve performance. If you do not believe me, try the following experiment. Eat a piece of fruit, then a candy bar separately, and pay attention to the effects on your mood. You will find that while both contain simple sugars, it is the glucose that makes the bigger impact on your system.

This goes to show the importance of glucose in providing quick energy. All while remembering that too much simple sugar can be detrimental to your health. Before any race, elite athletes calculate and optimize the levels of glucose their bodies can sustain. Experimenting with your body and finding the foods that fuel your fitness goals are a fun part of turning exercise into a lifestyle. I have even incorporated eating into my exercise routine to get the most out of my workouts. Fructose is the sugar found primarily in fruits, but it does not behave like other carbohydrates. Unlike other simple carbohydrates, fructose is not broken down quickly and is absorbed into the bloodstream. Instead, it stays in the liver and gets filtered for longer periods of time. This prolonged digestion can lead to spikes in insulin levels that may be harmful to long-term health.

The differences between all these sugars do not stop here. In fact, their abilities and applications can differ even further depending on the specific combination of glucose molecules. Sucrose, for example, which is the combination of glucose and fructose, makes up the most refined sugars that we consume in our daily lives. Lactose, which is composed of combined glucose and galactose, is an additive found in many dairy products. Finally, maltose, which is two forms of glucose combined, can be found in certain types of alcohol. While all sugars have their unique properties and applications, it is important to remember that they are a part of our daily lives and necessary for sustaining life.

Complex carbohydrates are a critical component of receiving the necessary levels of energy for any exercise. They can be divided into three categories: starches, fibers, and glycogen. Fibers are indigestible by humans, but their function is crucial for maintaining smooth digestion. They absorb water as they pass through the digestive tract, collecting residue on their way out. If you are suffering from constipation, increasing your intake of fiber might be a helpful solution. Fibers can be found in most whole grains, fruits, vegetable legumes, and nuts. Starches come from plants and are analogs to glycogen in the sense that they are reserve molecules. Finally, glycogen is found in animal muscles and liver and not in plants. However, it is also in microorganisms such as fungi and bacteria.

The most important thing to remember is that different carbohydrates have distinct functions, so it is important to know what works best for you and your health needs. By understanding the types of carbs available, you can make better choices to fuel yourself properly and keep your body running smoothly.

Protein

The importance of protein cannot be overlooked when it comes to keeping your body healthy. Protein is the fundamental building block of all life, and we depend on them for basic functions like digesting food, transporting oxygen throughout our bodies, repairing damage, and fighting infections. These thousands of proteins are composed of organic molecules called amino acids. Our bodies use twenty naturally occurring amino acids to create proteins. Of these, nine are not produced by our bodies, so we must obtain them from food sources.

Proteins are formed when these amino acids link together in a linear pattern, forming polypeptides. Each amino acid has a unique structure and composition, so the order in which they link together affects the shape and function of the protein. This means that proteins can be created in a variety of ways to achieve specific functions, such as transporting oxygen or storing energy.

Proteins are made up of amino acid chains that have distinct structures and can be classified into several types: structural, defense, hormonal, receptor, storage, enzymatic, and contractile proteins. Each type has its unique set of properties that determine how it works within the body. Structural proteins provide support and structure within the body, while defense proteins ward off invaders such as viruses and bacteria. As previously mentioned, hormonal proteins function as chemical messengers, while receptor proteins detect various signals from our environment. Storage proteins store energy for later use, enzymatic proteins catalyze chemical reactions, and contractile proteins facilitate movement. These diverse types of proteins serve a variety of purposes within our bodies to keep us functioning optimally.

All with distinct structures and properties that allow them to be arranged into so many different configurations, we can think of each amino acid as an exquisitely shaped molecular puzzle piece. When these pieces come together in the right order, we have a protein molecule perfectly suited for its designated purpose. While it is not necessary to know the details about all twenty amino acids and their functions, understanding how they work together is important. Having a basic understanding of how they interact can help you make better decisions when it comes to nutrition and health. By being more familiar with their functions, you can better nourish your body with the correct foods and nutrients. Knowing what type of protein you are looking for ahead of time can save a lot of energy in terms of trial and error. You may find yourself in a supplement store overwhelmed with all the different types of amino acids and proteins. However, if you have an idea of what works best for your body, then it can help narrow down your choices. Plant-based proteins might seem like the obvious healthy option. But if you have food intolerances to certain ingredients, like soya, for instance, then it is wise to steer clear from that selection. Knowing what type of protein works best for you will be beneficial not only when shopping around in the supplement store but also when formulating meal plans and creating recipes. Being informed about these types of proteins and amino acids is the key to unlocking a healthier, more nourishing lifestyle. Take the time to research what your body needs, and you may be rewarded with better health in return.

Our protein requirements depend on our size, activity levels, and goals. For example, athletes or those who engage in regular physical activity need more protein than those with sedentary lifestyles since their bodies need to repair damaged muscle tissue after strenuous exercise. Furthermore, consuming protein throughout the day can help support muscle growth and offer numerous other health benefits.

For people who are searching for alternative protein sources, there are a variety of options that can satisfy their needs. Vegan proteins such as legumes, nuts, and seeds are excellent sources of protein that can be easily digested. For example, chickpeas, lentils, tofu, soybeans, and tempeh can be great alternatives to animal-based proteins. While tempeh may not be the most popular vegan protein choice due to its unique flavor and texture, it is still a reliable source of high-quality protein.

Ultimately, it is important to focus on quality rather than quantity when selecting sources of protein. High-quality protein ensures that your body is getting all the essential amino acids it needs. Consuming protein immediately after exercise can help with muscle building and toning. Doing so will provide a useful source of energy for your body and aid in muscle recovery. Eating the right amount of quality protein every day can significantly improve your health and well-being.

Nucleic Acid

Nucleic acids are some of the most important macromolecules in existence, performing vital functions within cells, such as directing protein synthesis, storing, processing genetic information, and creating energy. Deoxyribonucleic acid and Ribonucleic acid, abbreviated DNA and RNA, respectively, are the two main classes of nucleic acids that naturally occur in all cells and even some viruses. Also, some artificial nucleic acids are produced synthetically for specific purposes and use in the medical industry, mainly research.

DNA is a double-stranded polymer composed of nucleotides, the building blocks of genetics, while RNA is its single-stranded counterpart. These nucleotides contain three components: a phosphate group, a sugar group, and a base group. A variety of several types of RNA exists, such as mRNA (messenger), rRNA (ribosomal), tRNA (transfer), and more. Messenger RNA is responsible for leaving the nucleus and delivering instructions to the cytoplasm, where proteins are assembled accordingly. Thus, it plays an instrumental role in protein synthesis by allowing genetic information to be stored, transmitted, and expressed. Overall, nucleic acids are essential for the continuation and maintenance of life, and without them, we simply could not exist.

The inner workings of DNA and RNA are incredibly complex. While you may not need to know all the intricate details, understanding the basic mechanisms of these macromolecules is essential to comprehending our unique destiny. We are each born with a set of genetic codes that dictates how our bodies build, develop, and operate, determining which nutrients we require, how our systems use them, and the way they are metabolized. From this cellular-level programming, our bodies create the proteins necessary for life, growth, and health. It is fascinating to think that the blueprint of who we are lies within our cells. It is these molecules that provide us with the power to shape our lives and find our place in the world.

It is important to understand that DNA does not determine an individual's fate but can certainly provide a framework for optimization. For example, a person with the DNA of an athlete may be more inclined to excel in physical activities such as sports or fitness. However, this does not mean that they cannot also develop an interest in books and literature or any other sedentary activity. The key is to recognize one's natural inclinations and use them to their best advantage. With the right combination of passion and effort, even those with seemingly insurmountable challenges can achieve remarkable things. It is up to the individual to recognize their strengths and weaknesses and use them to reach their goals. In this way, our DNA can be seen as a starting point rather than a limitation.

Lipids

Lipids are a macromolecule that most of us know as fat. We might think of fat in terms of excess weight and poor health. Although, in most cases, this might be true, it can also be much more than just an aesthetic aspect of our life. Fat is an important fuel source for our bodies, helping to provide long-lasting energy levels throughout our daily activities. It is essential to get the right kind of lipids into your system to make sure you have enough energy throughout the day. Not getting enough lipids can lead to fatigue and a lack of energy.

When it comes to fats, there are several types, and they each have their specific characteristics.

Unsaturated fats have the potential to reduce inflammation, improve heart health and provide essential fuel for our bodies. Foods like avocados, olives, and nuts are useful sources of unsaturated fats and should be included in a balanced diet.

Trans-fat is a type of unsaturated fat that is created through a chemical process. These manufactured fats are used for a variety of food products because they are cheaper to produce than other fats and have a long shelf-life. While it is true that trans-fat has these benefits, it also carries with it potential health risks.

Saturated fat has gotten a bad reputation over the years, but it is important to remember that not all saturated fats are created equal. Some saturated fats are essential nutrients that improve cardiovascular health and help regulate hormones. While it is true that eating too much-saturated fat can be unhealthy, it is important to remember that balance is key.

Coconut oil, palm oil, and cocoa butter are examples of saturated fats that can be beneficial to your health in moderation.

Phospholipids are another type of fat that forms the basis for cell membranes. They are composed of two fatty acids linked to a phosphate group. We can get our daily intake of phospholipids by consuming cereal grains and oilseeds such as soybeans, sunflower, and flaxseed. These foods not only help to regulate cholesterol levels, but they are also important for healthy brain and nervous system functioning.

Omega 3 fatty acids are a vital source of nutrition that we must obtain from outside sources, as our bodies cannot produce them naturally. To obtain these necessary fats, food sources such as flaxseed, chia seeds, and walnuts provide a reliable source of omega-3 fatty acids. Cholesterol and lipid hormones are classified as steroids, but they have different properties. Some cholesterol is essential for the body to create hormones and other substances, while other types of cholesterol can increase risk factors for heart disease. Lipid hormones are also important in regulating metabolism and immune system functions. It is important to understand the diverse types of fats and their properties to optimize health.

There is still a lot of confusion and misinformation about dietary fats. It is important to understand their unique role in the human body and how they can be used to reach your goals, whether that is gaining muscle mass, improving endurance performance, or simply staying healthy. So before demonizing all fats and cutting them from your diet, it is important to learn how you can use them as a powerful tool for achieving optimal health.

The Keto diet has been gaining a lot of attention lately. This high-fat, low-carbohydrate diet is said to trigger your metabolism so that it burns fat more efficiently and puts you into ketosis. This is a metabolic state in which ketones become an important source of energy for the body and brain. While this can be beneficial in the short term, in my opinion, this process can be dangerous if not monitored closely. You are essentially depriving your body of carbohydrates, which are essential for many bodily functions. Additionally, it is possible that you may lose weight during the period following this diet but gain more afterward. Therefore, consider your body requirements by analyzing your ultimate outcome. When it comes to racing triathlon, one size does not fit all. A person's physical weight is only relevant in the context of their objectives. Assuming that lighter bodies are always better for a triathlon is a supposition that ignores the reality that everyone has unique needs. So rather than shaming those who do not fit the traditional definition of an ideal triathlete body, it is more beneficial to celebrate everyone's unique approach to the sport. That way, we can all benefit from everyone's dedication to their training regimen.

We could also look at the case between Kristian Blummenfelt and Ben Kanute as prime examples of how professional athletes require distinct kinds of fuel sources. Kristian's critics thought that being seemingly overweight was incompatible with being a triathlete, yet he proved them wrong. Kristian is an Olympic champion, world record holder, and winner of many Ironman championships who, in my opinion, seems to be using mainly lipids over carbohydrates to fuel his races and enhance his recovery process.

This has clearly worked for him since he was able to overtake Ben Kanute on the run during the 2022 Ironman 70.3 World Championship. This occurred even though Ben had a much slimmer body which would suggest that carbs are the primary source of his energetic demands. As such, we should be cautious not to generalize our views on athletes based on observed physical appearances alone. But instead, look beyond them and consider their actual performance.

Kristian is a notable example of how you do not have to be an athlete with the "ideal" body type to succeed. By utilizing his unique approach, I assume that Kristian has discovered that adding fat to his diet helps sustain energy levels and allows him to recover sooner after strenuous exercise. This approach has enabled him to do an impressive number of races in any given year.

Nutritional choices

Everyone should strive to be aware of their nutritional requirements. To account for this, it is important to pay attention to how your body responds to distinct types of foods and adjust accordingly. I believe that the best way to do this is by keeping a food journal and tracking how you feel after eating certain meals. This can guide you toward an optimal diet tailored specifically to your body's needs. Ultimately, it is important to realize that everyone is different, and you should take the time to find out what works for you nutritionally.

When it comes to nutritional advice, the best words of wisdom I ever heard were from a documentary about a bodybuilder who swam the entire circumference of England. He started with a muscular body shape and believed he would lose weight during his journey. Instead, Ross Edgley ended up with much more weight.

What was so impressive about this feat was not just the remarkable physical accomplishment but also the insight he gained into nutrition and bodybuilding. His advice to others was simple: shape your body and nutrition for your purpose. After all, everyone's needs are different. What works for one person may not necessarily be best for another. In other words, an endurance athlete has different physical demands than a sprinter.

You do not have to be superhuman or live on some strange diet. You can make smart, conscious decisions that will benefit you. However, these decisions should not be extreme. For example, while drinking Cool aid may not be the healthiest choice out there, it is not necessarily a horrible behavior if done in moderation. On the other hand, substituting your entire food and beverage intake for an extended period with this sugary drink is certainly not a wise decision. Similarly, eating only one fruit for months may not be the healthiest alternative.

Instead of looking for radical diets and fads, focus on healthy behaviors like eating a variety of nutritious foods, getting regular exercise, and managing stress levels effectively. These are small steps that can lead to substantial changes in the long run. Health should always be a priority no matter what path you choose to take.

We are conditioned to want certain types of foods based on the cues our environment provides. The fact that we now live in an overabundance of food means that it is far too easy for us to indulge in unhealthy cravings when what we need is nutritious, balanced meals. If you can recognize this and make a conscious effort to resist your cravings, then you are taking control of your diet and setting yourself up for a healthier future. For example, if you find yourself wanting a donut despite knowing it is not the best for you — ask yourself why? Is it because you are hungry, or is it simply because donuts contain considerable amounts of sugar and lipids which your body has been conditioned to crave?

When it comes to an understanding of how you should approach any food in relation to your overall well-being, remember that you can break down the craving into the aforementioned macronutrient, protein, lipid, and carbohydrate. If what your body is really after is lipids, then perhaps instead of getting the sugars attached to them in their current donut form, you could look for alternatives to get those same lipids without taking on all the energy-sapping sugars.

A wise alternative might be to put a small amount of sunflower oil into your favorite cup of tea after supper. That way, you would be left feeling both satisfied and more energetic than if you had just eaten the complete dessert. In the end, indulging your taste buds can be an equally important part of creating a happy relationship with food. With a little practice and effort, you can learn how to make conscious decisions about what you eat rather than being swayed by the ever-present marketing propaganda of the food industry. With this approach, your eating habits can become both nutritious and delicious!

One anecdote with my son may have been simple, but it speaks volumes about the power of food in our lives. After what could be hours of exhaustive physical activity, I would usually ingest an excessive amount of food that was comical even to him. On my son's ninth birthday, I brought him to the grocery store to buy a cake. As I watched him add a second cake to our shopping cart, I questioned him about this sudden addition. He answered that the first cake was to celebrate his special day, and the second was to prevent me from eating all his cake. He knew that eating several desserts was a piece of cake for me: or two!

All jokes aside, sodium and sugar have long been demonized for their "unhealthy" reputation, but the truth is that both can be essential to peak performance. Used in the right context, sodium, and sugar can be invaluable components of your diet. For instance, sodium helps nerve impulses travel along their pathways while also maintaining proper fluid balance. Similarly, sugar provides a convenient source of energy to fuel your body and can help restore glycogen levels in the muscles after a hard workout. In short, do not be too quick to dismiss sodium and sugar. Used properly, they have much to offer.

Overall healthy regime

The idea of a balanced diet is often thrown around. However, what constitutes a balanced diet can really be subjective. Each person's dietary needs depend on their physical and mental health, fitness goals, lifestyle habits, dietary preferences, and environmental factors like geography. After all, when it comes to optimizing your athletic performance, a suitable regime is essential. A well-adjusted food plan tailored to meet your specific necessities should be the foundation of any successful training program.

Humans have incredible potential to expend more energy than they can consume. Therefore, start pushing yourself, and you will soon be burning much higher amounts of calories each day. Awareness of calorie counting may be useful to establish a baseline level of understanding and can be used as an educational tool. However, more than a numbers game, it is even more important to consider the quality of calories consumed.

Do not get fooled by thinking that vegans or any other types of diets are healthier. Most health-conscious individuals do not realize that some precious fruits and vegetables have fillers or colorants on them. A lot of plant-based food is also genetically modified to fill your belly. The idea is to understand that certain types of food create inflammation in your body, depending on certain body types. You must be aware of what you are eating and the effects it has on your body.

It is essential that we focus on the individual and the purpose when it comes to nutrition. What works for one person may be completely wrong for another, depending on their size, activity level, age, and health condition. For instance, a 500 lbs. person needs more food than just celery to meet their caloric requirements and stay healthy. It is important to take the individual's needs into consideration, as well as their preferences when creating a diet plan. This way, we can ensure that the person will be getting all the nutrients that they need to stay healthy and strong. Only then can we have an optimal outcome for everyone?

Intermittent Fasting

Fasting is a powerful tool to reset your body and mind. It has been practiced since ancient times, and its benefits have been demonstrated in multiple studies. When you stop eating for 8 hours or more, your body enters a state of fasting where it begins to return to its original hormonal state. By committing to a regular fasting routine, you can unlock the potential for improved mental clarity and focus, better sleep quality, and even weight loss.

It is always wise to consult with a healthcare professional before making any drastic changes in your routine. With the right guidance and knowledge, fasting can be an incredibly useful tool for improving your health and well-being.

With the right guidance, fasting can help boost metabolism, improve heart health, increase longevity, reduce inflammation that occurs with food intake, and even positively affect brain function and mood. Furthermore, it helps to improve body composition and steroid levels in the body, making it a great option for those looking to gain lean muscle mass and strength.

Additionally, eating late at night can be detrimental to your sleep quality and mental focus. To ensure that your body has enough time to digest before you fall asleep, try playing around with the timing of when you eat. If you have a fast metabolism, consider eating no more than one hour before bedtime. On the other hand, if you have a slow metabolism, it may be wise to stop eating 4 hours before sleep. This will help make sure that your body has finished metabolizing your food by the time you hit the pillow and thus reduce indigestion-related issues. Having an optimal schedule for eating can allow room for better mental clarity during the day and quality rest at night.

The key to healthy living is not about following a diet. It is about developing lifestyle habits that are sustainable rather than trying to fix a problem with a temporary solution. The reality is that most people do not need to go on a crash diet to live a healthier life. All it takes is making small adjustments to your current eating and exercise habits.

Fueling beyond nutrition

To fuel our bodies is far more than simply a matter of food. It is an entire process that involves both the physical and mental realms of our existence. Anything that you allow into your mind has a tremendous impact on how you perform. It is not only the food and liquids you ingest but also the conversations, movies, images, music, and any other type of stimulation that may enter your body. For instance, athletes who listen to exciting music while working out will typically see an increase in performance.

Similarly, conflicts in conversation or unfortunate life events may cause a decrease in execution due to a negative emotional state. Therefore, it is important to be mindful of what goes into your body as it directly affects how well you can operate. In essence, everything that flows into your organic structure serves as brainpower. Choose wisely! Reading books can be a fantastic way to feed your mind. It is so much better than relying on electronic devices unless you have a medical diagnosis that requires it. Even if you just read one page per day, it can help to keep your brain active and fueled with knowledge. Also, looking at a real book puts much less strain on your eyes than looking at a computer screen. So, the next time you want to learn something or stay sharp, consider cracking open an enjoyable book.

Chapter 5: Body Work

"Life is a balance between rest and work. Know your limits and play accordingly."

~JD

Your body is much more than a well-built engine; it is a multitude of incredible systems that needs to be cared for and maintained properly. Many exercises exist to help you look after your body. However, it is equally important to listen to its needs and be mindful of the stresses placed upon it. Finding an activity that reduces stress while still providing physical benefits is essential.

Our musculoskeletal system is a crucial component of our overall health, and taking care of it is essential for our well-being. Physical activity can be beneficial if done in moderation and tailored to your needs. Not only will you enjoy the physical benefits of improved balance, coordination, and strength, but movement can also give you a mental boost. Well-structured physical activity can improve your attention, concentration, and focus, enhance mental sharpness, reduce stress and anxiety, and increase endorphin levels. Regular physical activity of any kind can help to improve your overall performance as an athlete.

Whether it is running, weightlifting, or swimming, having a consistent routine that is tailored to you and your goals will lead to better results. With increased enthusiasm for exercise comes improved motivation, pushing you toward greater success in the long run. It is no secret that physical activity can have a positive impact on your performance, both in the short term and long term. Whether you are just starting as an athlete or are looking to take your performance to the next level, remember movement is key. Invest in yourself and make it a priority to stay active. You will thank yourself later.

The following are crucial benefits of movement and pain control that may help enhance the performance of an athlete.

Pain or Discomfort

When undergoing a challenge such as a triathlon, it is important to recognize the distinction between pain and discomfort. Pain is simply an indicator that something is wrong. Continuing could cause damage or be dangerous. On the other hand, discomfort should not be seen as something to fear or be avoided. It can often signal the presence of an opportunity for growth and improvement that we would have otherwise missed. True pain is often an indication that your body seriously needs attention, whereas uncomfortable growth is more in line with pushing your boundaries beyond the normal range.

Such as in muscle growth, discomfort is a necessary part of the process. When the connective tissue around our muscles gets damaged while exercising may not be pleasant, it is an essential factor in creating the change that you desire. Muscle soreness is a sign that you are pushing your body and making progress. The more you put in, the greater the outcome will be. So, embrace the soreness and let it be a reminder that you are doing something good for yourself. The same can be applied to other areas of life. If you are looking to make a momentous change in your life, it is likely going to be uncomfortable. You may need to push yourself out of your comfort zone and take risks that you would not normally take. But by doing so, you are allowing yourself to grow and achieve the goals that you have set for yourself.

During my experience, I felt immense discomfort throughout the Epicdeca, but I knew it was a necessary part of the process. Rather than giving up, I took extended periods of rest in transition to get my body and mind back in the right place before tackling the next challenge. In doing so, I was able to find a balance between pushing through and understanding when to take a break. Making an effort to reach your healthy living goals, even while dealing with discomfort in any part of your body, can be difficult. However, evidence-based treatments such as exercise can not only help you to manage the condition but also provide temporary relief. It is important that you consult a professional when attempting this approach so you know what exercises are safe and effective for your specific condition.

CHAPTER 5: BODY WORK

Pressure Points

Pressure points are an ancient and highly effective technique used by martial artists, soldiers, assassins, and others to improve their physical ability or take away life. Acupoints can also be a powerful form of healing and self-care, long used in traditional Asian medicine to stimulate the body's healing mechanisms and to promote well-being. While not a substitute for medical advice or form of any diagnosis, these simple exercises can help manage stress, ease tension, and reduce pain. They are also wonderful ways to focus your attention on the present moment and build awareness of your body's energy levels.

These hundreds of acupoints, or energy points, can be connected through a network of pathways known as "meridians." Each meridian is associated with a particular organ system, providing a way for the energy to flow through the body and nourish the organs. This network of energy is constantly circulating throughout the body, and when there is an imbalance or blockage in the flow of energy, this can lead to physical and emotional health problems. By stimulating key points along the meridians, acupoints may help reduce inflammation and tension while encouraging relaxation and improving overall well-being.

To get started, simply choose an acupoint that is correlated with the outcome you are looking for. Once you have found a spot that feels more sensitive than the surrounding area, that is probably the location of your trigger point.

Then, using your finger, gently stimulate the area using circular or up-and-down movements. Be mindful of the sensation you feel and breathe deeply as you keep your eyes closed. As you do this exercise, you may notice that various parts of your body start to relax. Allow your body to sink into the relaxed state that comes from being in a calm and centered state of mind. With regular practice, you can begin to use these acupoint exercises as a tool for self-care and growth. If you believe that acupressure may be beneficial for you, I strongly recommend that you seek out a qualified acupuncturist or practitioner with expertise in this field.

I have learned over the years how to use certain pressure points to help alleviate unwanted discomfort in my body. For example, one of the most beneficial points that help with anxiety is in between your eyebrows. This helped calm my system and reduced feelings of anxiety.

Another pressure point that has been extremely useful for me is the one between the thumb and index finger on my dominant hand. This point has been great for dealing with my stress, as it had a calming effect on my body. The use of this acupressure point was a terrific way to discreetly manage stress amid any situation. I was able to utilize this method without anyone noticing, simply by concealing my hand during meetings or dinner table conversations.

Finally, another pressure point that I use is the one above the sternum in the middle of my chest. This particular pressure point has helped me deal with emotional stress and increased my feelings of well-being.

It is important to note that these pressure points are not without risks. Some of them may induce labor, so make sure to use caution when using them if you are pregnant. When it comes to dealing with discomfort, I have found that pressure points can be a highly effective way of alleviating some of the symptoms. Of course, there are so many other pressure points and techniques to explore when it comes to acupressure. However, these are not magically rapid cures and should always be used in combination with other approaches such as exercise, nutrition, and relaxation. Acupressure massage can be a powerful and effective tool for addressing chronic conditions, but it is important to remember that its effectiveness can vary significantly depending on the individual. A healthcare professional will be able to provide tailored advice and treatment based on your specific needs, so it is important to speak with them before beginning any acupressure massage routine.

Massage Therapy

If you are looking to relieve stress, improve your posture or just relax, considering massage therapy may be a great option for you. Massage therapy can be a powerful addition to your exercise routine. Not only does massage work as a stress reliever, but it also helps restore circulation in areas of your body that may have been strained or impacted during physical activity. Regular massage sessions can help your body heal faster and improve mobility, allowing you to get back into the swing of things more quickly. For athletes, massage therapy can also help prevent injuries and reduce the risk of any future ones from occurring.

Massage therapy is a powerful form of medical treatment that can provide profound results in a variety of conditions. However, it is important to remember that the quality of massage therapy offered varies widely depending on where you get it done. Make sure to research and select a qualified practitioner who specializes in the type of massage that best suits your needs.

Massage boots are a great investment for anyone looking to save money on massage therapy. While they are not as comprehensive or effective as an experienced therapist, the benefits of these boots can still be felt when used in conjunction with regular massage. One of my favorite financial decisions was buying massage boots while I was in Texas. Not only did it save me money in the long term, but it also allowed me to experience a level of relaxation and recovery that I would not have been able to during the Epicdeca. Plus, the ease of use and convenience of massage boots meant that anyone could use them.

I find it amusing to bring my massage boots on planes as a carry-on item. It is certainly not something you see every day at the airport, and I always get a kick out of seeing the security guard's expression as they open my bag and ask me what it is.

Posture

The importance of proper posture in our daily life should not be underestimated. Good posture helps us to maintain an upright spine and prevents problems like back pain, neck pain, and headaches. It also allows our muscles to work more efficiently so we can remain energized throughout the day. Developing good habits from an early age will help ensure that you have good posture when you get older. Posture can also affect our confidence levels as it affects how we stand and carry ourselves.

Therefore, focusing on improving our posture can help us to boost our self-esteem. Finally, having a good posture allows for more efficient breathing, which improves oxygen flow to the brain and provides us with more energy.

Being aware of good posture is essential to your health and well-being. Your feet are the foundation of your whole body, so it is important to make sure you get the right type of shoes for the sport or activity that you are doing. When I was a kid, I used to work hard so I could buy myself new shoes all the time. Even though I did not understand why at the time, I now recognize why it is important to make sure your footwear is right for what you are doing.

Posture can also apply to other sports, such as cycling. When you are starting cycling, one of the most important things to do is make sure that your bike is properly fitted. This means adjusting the saddle height, handlebar position, and other aspects so that they fit correctly. Not only will this ensure that you feel comfortable while riding, but it will also help to reduce injuries and improve your performance.

In recent years, one of most people's guilty pleasures is spending too much time glued to their phones. We get caught up in a digital world, and before we know it, hours have gone by without us having moved an inch. While this may seem harmless enough, what we do not realize is that this form of distraction puts us into an awake coma that keeps us inactive for hours. Our bodies need movement to stay healthy, and when we do not give them what they need, we start to feel aches and pains that may never go away. This pain can radiate to other parts of our body, leaving us worse off than before.

Active Recovery

A day of active recovery can be the perfect way to give your body a break from intense training while still providing some beneficial movement. Focusing on low to moderate-intensity exercises will help keep you energized and prevent exhaustion. It is important to remember that the goal during an active recovery day is not to push yourself too hard; rather, it is to maintain a relaxed state and allow your body to rest. This could include activities such as gentle stretching, a leisurely walk, or even something fun like a Zumba class. Whatever activity you choose, keep it light and focus on giving your body the rest it needs.

Taking a day of active recovery is as important to your body's health and performance as regular exercise. Increased blood flow to the muscles, tissues, and other parts of the body helps deliver essential nutrients that allow for musculoskeletal repair. Additionally, active-recovery exercises can help reduce the buildup of lactic acid and hydrogen ions that cause tiredness in the muscles.

Stretching can be an effective way to reduce muscle soreness caused by physical training. Several types of stretching have diverse applications, including ballistic, dynamic, active, passive, static, and isometric. If you are looking to relieve yourself from minor muscular aches and pains, then gently stretching the affected muscles can do a world of good. When stretching, it is important to understand the difference between pain and discomfort. Aim for a slight feeling of tension, but never push your body too far to the point of pain. Hold each stretch for several seconds, and be sure to focus on your breathing throughout the process. With regular stretching, you will be able to improve your flexibility and reduce muscle soreness.

Controlled movement and stretching have amazing benefits for our bodies, extending far beyond just physical well-being. Studies have shown that regular exercise can positively affect hormone levels. So, if you are looking to optimize your hormones naturally and are curious about what the best approach is, I recommend doing some research into which hormones you are targeting and seeking out scholarly articles on the subject.

CHAPTER 5: BODY WORK

Cold Water

Cold water is a powerful tool to reduce inflammation in the body. It helps to heal sore muscles, soothe arthritic joints, and can even help with headaches. Cold water immersion therapy has been used for centuries as an effective remedy for pain relief, and modern research is showing it to be an effective way of treating many chronic conditions. Taking a cold shower or immersing yourself in freezing water is a natural way to reduce inflammation and improve overall health. It can also help to ease stress and anxiety, boost your mood, and restore balance in your hormonal state.

The first few seconds of submerging into chilly water can be the most difficult challenge. The human body has an incredible capacity to adjust and acclimate itself to changing environments, and this includes extreme temperatures. After those initial few seconds, your body will begin to regulate its core temperature to maintain a comfortable level for you. It is an amazing feat of biology and endurance that should not be taken for granted. With perseverance and dedication, you can train your body to become accustomed to the coldness and enjoy the health benefits that come along with it.

The best method for cold water therapy is to use fresh water from a lake or waterfall. A modern times alternate method to gain the same benefits as a natural cascade is to use a bathtub filled with a mixture of water and ice. Instead of submerging yourself in a cold bath, you can turn on the hot water in your shower and then switch to cold for a few seconds. Doing this regularly will allow you to train your body to sustain cold temperatures longer over time without the logistics and cost of filling up a tub.

Susanna Soberg's 11/57 method of cold-water therapy provides an elegant framework for the regular practice of this ancient healing technique. According to her research, submerging yourself up to the neck in cold water for eleven minutes per week can lead to profound physical and psychological benefits. While the science behind this method is still being understood, research suggests that exposure to freezing water can have positive effects on brown fat and dopamine levels and even reduce the body's sensitivity to cold temperatures. Susanna Soberg's work on cold water therapy is a revelation, and it is a shame I did not come across it before I conducted so many of my experiments with cold-snow immersion in my underwear. To learn more about the advantages of this technique, I recommend seeking out Susanna's book "Winter Swimming."

After conducting my experiments, I found that cold water therapy was a remarkably effective way to alleviate muscle pain and reduce swelling. Submerging only the affected part of the body in freezing water brought about speedy relief from the tenderness. For example, during the Epicdeca challenge, my crew carried a bucket that contained a mixture of water and ice. Whenever I experienced pain or swelling, I would take a break and submerge the affected area in the freezing water. This provided me with targeted relief from my discomfort, which was incredibly helpful in keeping me going throughout the challenge.

Family Recovery

I define family recovery as utilizing the close relationships in our lives and taking steps to nurture them to recover from the stressors of life. It is easy to become overwhelmed when faced with life's challenges but remember that we are not alone. We all have some form of family and loved ones who can provide us with the support and comfort to help us get through any difficulty. You may not be aware, but this can be our biological family, as well as our friends, colleagues, and mentors.

When it comes to recovering from stress, the family may not be the first thing that comes to mind. For some, the family can be a source of stress, and the idea of turning to them for help may seem counterintuitive. However, it is important to recognize that family relationships can be powerful sources of strength and healing, provided we approach them with the right attitude.

We all have a responsibility to ourselves, as well as our families, to be mindful of our thoughts and actions. It is easy for us to fall into patterns of negativity, but when we do this, it can create a ripple effect of destructive energy that affects our partners and children. To avoid this, try to find ways to reframe your understanding of family dynamics and replace negative thoughts with positive ones.

Focus on finding the good in your family and celebrating their capabilities rather than fixating on what is wrong. Remember that our families are made up of individuals with unique talents and personalities, and while they may clash sometimes, that does not mean they cannot also help one another.

Also, it can be helpful to distance yourself from problematic family members. It may be difficult to do this, but sometimes it is necessary in order to maintain your mental health and well-being. Disengage from negative family dynamics and focus on the positive aspects of your relationship.

To some, this mental transformation can be the most challenging one to undertake. In our modern society, where we are increasingly separated from family, we tend to let our hate toward former partners' fester. We may find comfort in our colleagues, consciously or unconsciously searching for new companionship, sometimes even involving physical contact. But we should never let hate lead us to selfish decisions because they will only bring suffering eventually.

Instead, a better approach to finding security and strength in relationships is to invest in training our neurotransmitters. This means learning and understanding how to navigate our relationships in a way that will be conducive to our recovery. It starts with being mindful of the stimuli we encounter and understanding how our body reacts to them. We need to learn to recognize which patterns are beneficial to our recovery, as well as which ones we should avoid.

The point is rooted in patience and kindness to create a healthy balance. The patience to understand that everyone has shortcomings and needs help to regain a healthy balance. Also, kindness creates compromise for everyone.

Relationships are complex and often require a lot of work. Here are some tips to help you improve your relationships.

Frequency

The unseen forces of the world are often overlooked, but they can be immensely powerful. We tend to take for granted that everything we experience is a frequency, from what we hear to what we choose to say. Words are a form of frequency, and they can be positively or negatively effective. We have the power to choose how we express ourselves, and those words carry an energy that can shape our reality. Similarly, each person has a frequency that is determined by their experiences and the energy they choose to hold on to. The more negative energy one holds onto or is subjected to, the more one hurts themselves and those around them. It is important to remember that no matter what kind of frequency you are receiving from someone else, it does not necessarily have to be reciprocated. Reacting destructively to negative energy only perpetuates the cycle and consequently causes more harm than good.

On the other hand, if we can choose to become aware of our frequency and focus on the positive, we may create a powerful force for good in our lives and those around us. We can make the world a better place by simply being mindful of our frequency and its influence. By recognizing the power of these vibrations, we can create ripple effects that will have a positive impact on the world.

Just as a radio station can be tuned in to certain frequencies, so too can our brains. These phenomena vary based on the time of day and even who is speaking. Understanding this concept can give us an incredible edge in being able to recognize the frequencies of the people around us, allowing us to make more powerful connections and create an even stronger positive energy in our lives. It is an innovative way to think about the world and a powerful tool for improving our lives.

So, next time you are listening to someone speak, take a moment to recognize the power of their words and the frequency you are experiencing. You may be surprised at how it can change the way you react. In my opinion, it is not that our attention spans are too short or that we are all suffering from an attention deficit epidemic; it is more a problem with how we deliver the material. We need to present information in a way that captures people's interest and focuses their attention on the task at hand. For example, have you ever wondered why you are able to focus for hours on every word your first lover said, yet when it comes to listening to a professor, you are ready to fall asleep within the first 10 minutes? This is largely due to the difference in frequency that everyone brings and how it is perceived. Likewise, you may be asleep in certain sections of this book and want more of other segments. By rereading this book later, you may find that the same portions that were once boring suddenly became enthralling. Therefore, using this book as an orientation can be beneficial, as it allows you to take in the different concepts on different days.

In many cases, the world has a lot of negative

energy that can be difficult to navigate. However, completely removing yourself from anything negative can do more harm than good. It is important to be aware of the environment and context in which you are operating so that you can develop the necessary skills to deal with situations and circumstances that may be difficult to process. By understanding the source of stress, anxiety, or negativity, you will be better equipped to manage such situations. Ultimately, by avoiding negative situations that might be causing distress, rather than completely removing yourself, you can be more emotionally mature and better prepared to navigate the world.

Love

In my opinion, this frequency is the most powerful in the world. It can make us feel alive, and it can drive us to heights we never thought possible. It can motivate us to do incredible things, but it can also be dangerous when we do not use it appropriately. To further understand the nature of love, we must consider the many facets and nuances of this emotion. Love can be found in acts of kindness and compassion, by being merciful and forgiving, and by being generous and loyal. It can also be found in simply being present and attentive to another person's needs. Love is a complex emotion that comes in many forms, and it can be used for both good and bad.

We should constantly evaluate our intentions and examine the motivations behind our actions, as this can have a tremendous impact on the outcome. Conversely, infatuation is not a type of love but more of a heightened, harmful feeling that can be dangerous. It can lead to unrealistic expectations and blinding emotions, which can cause us to make bad decisions and go against our values. True love is built upon trust and understanding. It is a feeling that grows over time with patience and nurture.

When it comes to love and addiction, it can be tempting to rely on others for help. However, it is important to remember that you are the only one who holds power to profoundly change your situation. Be mindful of the fact that not all help comes from good intentions, and it is important to know when it is time to walk away from a situation that may be harmful or even illegal. It is only through taking ownership of your addiction and pushing yourself to make difficult but rewarding changes that you can achieve true growth. Many people can be part of your journey to recovery, but you must remain in the driver's seat and make sure that they are truly helping you.

In the end, you must have a loose grip on your relationships to exhibit your love. If you cannot let go and accept that the outcome is not always in your control, then you never really had a healthy relationship with the person in the first place. Learning to let go is a key step in achieving loving connections.

Confidence

When a person radiates a sense of self-assurance, it is often felt by those in their immediate vicinity. People are drawn to those with the inner strength and courage to tackle life's challenges head-on. Do not be disheartened if your progress along the journey of success is slower than you anticipated. We all start from different points and travel at various speeds. Instead of giving up and lamenting, take the challenges presented to you in stride and remain hungry for more. It is easy to recognize someone who is confident and successful. They do not need to brag but show it through their actions. This is the mindset of a person who is hungry for more, and it can be trained. It is not a matter of faking confidence but developing it through consistent effort and dedication.

As an example, the difference between normal soldiers and special forces personnel lies primarily in the frequency with which they practice their skills and the degree of focus that is applied. Special forces personnel are accustomed to performing the same task repeatedly and with a greater intensity of focus than the average infantry soldier. This brings about assurance and proficiency in the skills needed, as well as allows them to react naturally in any given situation. Conversely, the ordinary soldier will perform tasks proficiently but with less instinctive ability. In this way, the special forces are better prepared for any circumstance they may be asked to perform. So do not be discouraged if you feel like others are passing you by — the path to success is a marathon, not a sprint. Be confident in your way and keep pushing forward.

People who have low self-esteem and are quick to judge you may feel threatened by your presence. This is why it is important for you to be aware of how you are coming across and to be as respectful as possible when interacting with them. After all, these people are struggling with their issues and insecurities, and your accomplishments are likely a reflection of their lack of success. That being said, you should never arrogantly use your triumphs, as this can just further aggravate the situation. Instead, focus on the positive and take responsibility for your actions.

In cases where someone may be over-compensating, it is important to remember that this is likely due to a lack of self-confidence. The person is trying to control the situation out of a need to be accepted and validated. This is why you should take a step back, remain calm and understand where they are coming from. You could also address the root of their behavior by listening to what they have to say and responding compassionately. All while considering that this approach does not excuse their behaviors or the eventuality that their worldview may be skewed and needs attention. However, by remaining confident, you can help them realize that their behaviors are not necessary for acceptance and validation.

Being aware of how you come across and how others may perceive your actions is key to avoiding situations of manipulation. This is especially true for those who are in positions of power. People can feel threatened even if you do not mean to be intimidating, and it is important to be mindful of how you interact with them when displaying your confidence.

Emotions

Facing our emotions and traumas can be the hardest thing we ever do in life. Additionally, it is essential to find ways to manage and channel these emotions in a balanced and healthy way that works for us. Everyone has separate ways of making sense of and dealing with their emotional world. Some people feel comfortable getting into a boxing ring with someone they trust and hitting each other in a safe and controlled environment. Others might opt for a more tranquil approach, like going for a long run to calm their mind. For others, they might seek out a space where they can take destructive objects and break them to find some kind of catharsis.

Whatever it is that resonates with you, you must find the right outlet for managing and containing your emotions as best as you can. Taking the time to find out what works for you will have long-term benefits and is an important practice for your physical, mental, and emotional well-being. The possibilities are truly endless. We must not demonize or ignore the diverse options available to us, as they can be powerful tools for managing our emotions. Through trial and error, you can find the right balance for yourself.

Although most emotions are frequencies, I wanted to cover confidence and love in a separate section, as those seem to be fundamental to achieving life goals. No matter how hard life gets, and no matter how much negative frequencies your brain throws at you, it is always within your power to choose a different response. We are in complete control of our actions, even if it does not always feel that way.

By understanding how and why your brain works the way it does, you can gain the tools to train yourself out of certain reactions that no longer serve you. Even if you have been behaving a certain way for years, it is never too late to explore more positive frequencies and potentially generate more progressive ripples in the world.

When it comes to emotions, we often tend to hide away or "put on a protective glove" to shield ourselves from what is happening. Doing so is a helpful safety mechanism in an emergency, but it can become destructive if we do this for a prolonged period. Instead, what is more important is how we react to the stimuli generated by an incident. While emotions can vary between people, it is essential that we healthily manage them and that we allow them to live and thrive in different environments. By taking the time to understand our emotions, rather than suppressing them, we can learn to become better equipped for handling demanding situations.

Start with small steps and continue to progress at whatever pace works for you. Emotional intelligence is a skill that can be honed, sharpened, and mastered. As you learn more about yourself, it will become easier to regulate your emotions and move in a positive direction. With the right resources and a little bit of effort, you can develop the ability to recognize and manage your feelings effectively. As you do this, you will be able to recognize triggers and find ways to channel them in a healthy, productive way. This will make it easier to stay focused and motivated in your endeavors. Do not be afraid to pick up a book on managing emotions or seek out therapy if you find yourself feeling overwhelmed. It is never too late to learn from your mistakes and grow in ways that can positively impact yourself and the world around you. So, stay hungry for more and keep learning.

Perspective

Our perspectives on life events will not always be shared by others. We must recognize this, as it can help us manage our expectations when interacting with others. We must explain our perspective, but we must also understand when it is not shared and be able to move on without expecting everyone to agree with us. We need to be respectful of other people's perspectives and allow them their space to view the world in the way that works best for them. When we are faced with different perspectives, our challenge is to find common ground or a way to bridge the divide in understanding. We can still learn from each other and grow from our differences. It is not easy, but it is important to keep a respectful attitude in order to reach a better understanding. It may take time, but the effort to bridge understanding is invaluable.

One concept that is often misunderstood is the idea that nobody can make us angry. We may be provoked or challenged by outside forces, but it is our thoughts that lead to an angry reaction. We must learn to control our thinking and understand the power that we have over our reactions. With this mindset, we can choose to not give in to negative thoughts and emotions, which will prevent us from reacting out of anger. This is a difficult concept to understand, but once it is grasped, we can notice the power that we have over our reactions.

It may take time and effort to master this concept, but when it is understood, we will always be able to look at the world with a unique perspective. If we remember that our actions derive from our thoughts, we may be on to a breakthrough. Instead of asking how the world changes around us, we need to ask how we can change ourselves, which will, in turn, change the world.

This is a hard concept, but one that can lead to a more successful and meaningful life. We live the life we have been conditioned to, but if we take a step back and examine our thought patterns, we can make slight changes that will bring about better results. When we take responsibility for our actions and understand the power we have over our thoughts, we can live the life we want. We can make the world a better place, one thought at a time.

Needs

It is essential to recognize the difference between a need and a want. When it comes to our everyday lives, we all have needs that must be fulfilled to ensure our survival and well-being. These include food, water, safety, shelter, and companionship. On the other hand, wants are desires that are not essential for survival, and they often come with a price. Whether it is buying a new car or taking an exotic vacation, it is important to remember that these wants are not necessary, and if they come at too high a cost, it can lead to an imbalanced lifestyle.

This, in turn, may cause a snowball effect, including mental health and having to compensate in other areas of our life. Living a fulfilling life means recognizing when a need is a need and when something is just a want. Only then will you be able to make sound decisions and lead a balanced life?

Wants can be extremely helpful in leading a fulfilling life, depending on how they are used. Wants can function as motivators, pushing us to strive for something better and giving us a sense of accomplishment when we reach our goals. But anything beyond our basic needs should be indulged in moderation and with full knowledge of the consequences. In this way, we can use our wants as stepping stones and be mindful of how they impact our mental health.

Mental needs should be taken as seriously as physical needs, and only by listening to our bodies and minds can we find solutions that work for us. Just because it is not always visible does not mean that it is not there. Take care of your mental health needs the same way you take care of your physical health, and you will be better equipped to tackle any challenge that comes your way.

Setting boundaries, even if they are temporary, can help you to stay focused and in control of the things that you can manage. Do not be afraid to step away from the news and other sources of negativity, even if only for a brief time. You have to take responsibility for your mental health, and that means making decisions that prioritize your well-being. Accepting that these changes may not be permanent can help you to find a way forward.

Excuses

Our experiences may feel limited, but they inform our thoughts, which then have an immense power to shape choices. Every decision we make impacts our behaviors for better or for worse. Those behaviors, large or small, have the capacity to shape our world in unexpected ways. This pattern of moving energy is, therefore, important to help us take responsibility for our choices and their consequences.

We must be mindful of how our actions affect not only ourselves but also those around us, for it is through this ripple effect that we can shape the world as a collective. Whether we realize it or not, our decisions have a far-reaching impact on the way our world looks and functions. By being aware of this power, we can use it responsibly to create lasting positive change and make a difference in our world.

Therefore, we must not allow excuses and avoidance of responsibility to get in the way of making a difference. Too often, we allow ourselves to be held back by fear and anxiety, and by crafting excuses, we hinder ourselves from achieving our goals. Regardless of how we feel, it is possible to start over and create a new path for ourselves. It is never too late to make a change for the better, and it is not about how much time has gone by or what mistakes we have made, but to act in the moment and keep striving forward. As coach Jeff used to tell me: "It is not about the beginning or the end, but rather the journey we take in between."

We must learn to take responsibility for our behavior and not make excuses. To do this, we need to be aware of the long-term consequences of our actions. We cannot just take refuge in the short-term comfort that comes from making excuses and blaming others, as this will only lead to further suffering. To take responsibility for our behavior is to be free and powerful.

We can choose how we respond to mistreatment rather than simply reacting out of habit. We can understand the patterns of our behaviors and take the necessary steps to break them to create positive change. If we choose to excuse ourselves from behaving in unproductive ways toward others only because we have been mistreated, then we are not truly exercising our freedom and power.

Instead, we are merely regurgitating the same emotions and behaviors that have kept us trapped in a cycle of negativity. This paradigm may also lead us to blame our system for poor hormonal secretion when it is our responsibility to break the cycle of abuse and create a healthier future. Otherwise, this ripple effect of negative behavior will continue to manifest itself in our lives and might also be creating subconscious anxiety as a result.

No matter how you were treated, it is never an excuse to respond in a derogatory or hurtful way. Choosing your response carefully and thoughtfully can lead to more productive conversations and better understanding between people. Encouraging others to also choose their words wisely can foster a positive atmosphere.

By choosing short-term convenience, we can sometimes end up on a path of least resistance through destructive behaviors. This type of avoidance is rarely beneficial overall and often masks underlying problems or issues that could be addressed more effectively. Bruce K. Alexander's Rat Park experiment is a prime example of this, and while it has contributed to our understanding of drug use, I disagree with his conclusion that the environment is solely responsible for addiction.

While it is true that changing the environment of a drug user can have a positive impact on their behavior, this is only part of the story. The Rat Park experiment failed to consider the influence of our daily responsibilities or that an environment can be anything other than perfect. For those unfamiliar with the experiment, Alexander placed rats in a cage with two bottles — one containing drugs and one water. The rat would go to the drug area more often than the water until he changed the environment of the rats by creating a giant rat park. As a result, the rats did not use the drugs and only drank water.

Although this experiment may have proven that environmental factors can play a role in addiction, it fails to address what happens when mistakes are made, or responsibilities are neglected. A perfect eutopia devoid of responsibilities and mistakes does not exist, nor should it. Life is meant to have a series of challenges and mistakes that can help us grow as individuals. To utterly understand addiction, we must consider a variety of issues that influence it, such as responsibilities, thought processes based on our experiences, and social dynamics. Only when we take all of these factors into account can we hope to produce effective solutions.

Ultimately, the key to overcoming addiction lies

within us. It is our responsibility to take ownership of our actions, learn from our mistakes, and not allow ourselves to fall prey to making excuses.

Support

Supporting yourself and others can have a powerful impact on your life and the lives of those around you. It is not always easy to do, but it can be incredibly rewarding. Even small acts of kindness can be effective and show that you are willing to help. By helping yourself, and then helping others, you can set an example for those around you. Support comes in many forms, and it can be expressed in a variety of ways.

The main two ways to support a person are by considering their needs and their perspective. Everyone needs distinct types of support, so it is important to be aware of what the person requires. Even if their perspective is contradictory or erroneous, we must see the situation objectively and aid in a way that meets their needs. It is not enough to simply shelter them or make excuses.

Support is an important part of growth and development. It can be difficult to navigate addiction, but with proper support, it can be done. Recovery takes time, and progress may not be seen immediately. So, set realistic expectations and be patient. That being said, there should always be a general trend of improvement in the person's behavior. If you feel like your help does not have the desired effect, it might be time to reassess your approach and make sure that you are helping rather than hindering.

Ultimately, the best way to support someone is to give them the tools and resources that they need. Show respect for their autonomy by allowing them to make decisions and choices. This will allow them to gain experience from their mistakes while also providing moral support. By allowing them to express themselves and make their decisions, you can provide the foundation for a positive future.

Support is a delicate balance, and it can be easy to get lost in need to control. You may feel like you are helping when, in fact, you are suffocating them with control. Always remember to support people in their endeavors, not by taking away their independence.

Finally, there is a long-standing misbelief that an apology is similar to an excuse. An apology is a way of recognizing one's wrongdoing or misdeed, whereas an excuse is simply attempting to justify the actions that were taken. An apology involves genuine humility, a recognition of the harm that has been done, and an acceptance of responsibility for it.

In some cases, apologies might be necessary. However, you must also recognize when an apology is not necessary and learn to stand up for yourself. It is all right to be wrong sometimes, but it is equally important to recognize when you are not in the wrong. Do not apologize simply to appease someone else, as it can set a precedent that an apology is required for every disagreement or dispute.

It is much better to take responsibility for any mistakes you have made and make a commitment to improving in the future rather than continuously apologizing for every mistake.

Continuous apologizing does not show signs of support but instead encourages poor behaviors to persist. In short, apologize when it is due and take responsibility for your actions without allowing yourself to be taken advantage of. Accept the situation and find a way to move past it. After all, the most important aspect is that we move away from our disagreements and reach an understanding.

Forgiving others for their wrongdoings is not always easy, but we should remember that everyone makes mistakes. Do not hold a grudge when the situation calls for resolution and understanding. It is often not about who is right or wrong but more about how we can work together to move forward. After all, the best way to move past a disagreement is when actions reflect apologies.

Family Recovery Summary

Family recovery is an ongoing process that can be used to your advantage. By constantly staying hungry and understanding that everyone has shortfalls, you may be on a path to success and use this to enhance your relationships.

By using the power of family connection, you could receive a healthy dose of oxytocin without having to search. You can also receive a negative side effect when your neurotransmitters are not reacting positively. Ultimately, you cannot change your partner or your family. Therefore, it is up to you to make the appropriate changes that you wish to see reflected in your relationships. So, take your partner on a date, take your children on outings, and allow them to play. Remain playful in your relationships. Show your partner and children that you appreciate them, show them love, and be patient with each other. This will benefit the entire family dynamic as it will create stability and understanding. It is important to forgive ourselves as well as others, everyone has made mistakes in the past, and this shall not define our present and future. Take the time to enjoy each other's company, have a meaningful conversation, make a goal together as a family, and work toward achieving this goal.

Family is one of the most valuable investments that a person can have, and with patience, understanding, and love, it might grow and become even stronger. It is not about being perfect and having nothing but good times. It is learning from mistakes and using those lessons to better ourselves and our families.

I am living proof that the best investment I have ever made was in myself and my relationship with my son. By making minor changes, even just spending more time together doing activities, we have grown closer. This has shaped our relationship in a way that I could not have imagined before.

So, instead of expecting others to make the changes you want to see, focus on yourself and the trivial things that can make a significant difference in your relationships. Give yourself and your family members the permission to grow together.

In conclusion, do not forget that you are all part of a team and that it is okay not to always have the answers. Showing your family members compassion, understanding, and love can go a long way in strengthening your relationships. Change is a process and not something that happens overnight, but if you have an open mind and stay focused on the goal, then you will be able to have successful relationships with your family. So, look at your problems with a unique perspective and start making the changes that you wish to see in yourself as well as in your family.

CHAPTER 5: BODY WORK

The topic of family recovery is a complex one, and I might have to create my next book about it.

Chapter 6: Rest

"Unless you document and apply,
you will do similar mistakes."

~JD

It was a difficult challenge to learn to take the time to rest and recover. I had become so accustomed to using workouts as a coping mechanism that it had become a crutch that I leaned on heavily. While this approach showed tremendous progress in my journey, it also became a double-edged sword when I started needing breaks from the intensity of exercise. Even after the Epicdeca was over and everyone had gone home, I still struggled with taking a break.

It took me some time to recognize my mistake in not giving myself permission to take a step back and take some time to rest. It was only then that I was able to put my needs of recovery first before anything else. This realization gave me the experiential knowledge to continue my education process toward a healthier lifestyle.

It is important to give your body time to rest between exercise sessions. Without this much-needed break, your body will not be able to repair itself and rebuild the muscle fibers you are working hard to strengthen. Even if you want to push yourself harder to reach your goals faster, it is important for recovery that you take breaks in between exercises. Recovery periods are necessary and beneficial in order to optimize the benefits of exercise. During these restful moments, your body is able to repair and rebuild the muscle tissue you have damaged during your workout session. Not only does this help you build strength, but it also helps prevent injuries from overworking muscles that have not had a chance to heal.

There is no one-size-fits-all answer that determines how much rest every person needs. Mainly because the amount of rest everyone requires will differ depending on their lifestyle, physical health, and mental well-being. For example, a Tour de France finisher typically takes at least three weeks off his feet with minimal stimulation. Whereas other individuals may need more or less time. It is important to take the time necessary for your body and mind to recover after intense exertion and remember to take relatively proportional rest based on your workout intensity.

Sleep

When we try to push ourselves too hard without rest, our bodies and minds suffer. Our mental health deteriorates, leading to greater stress and fatigue, which ultimately affects our productivity. When it comes to getting enough sleep, quality matters more than anything else. By taking the time to get adequate snoozes, our minds can refresh and rejuvenate, enabling us to better manage our daily tasks and responsibilities.

Rest and sleep are two vastly different yet equally

important aspects of our mental, emotional, and physical well-being. Rest is a period of relaxation or pause during which you do not engage in activities or exert effort. It can be active or passive and is essential for restoring energy and preventing burnout. Sleep, on the other hand, is a period of extended unconsciousness in which our body repairs and renews itself. Both rest and sleep are vital for maintaining a healthy, balanced lifestyle.

The type of rest you undertake is only part of the equation. It is important to remember that rest can come in many different forms and offer us a variety of benefits. Active rest, such as a brisk walk outdoors, can help to clear your head and give you some much-needed fresh air. Passive rest, on the other hand, such as taking 10 minutes a day to sit down and relax, can help you to recenter yourself, reflect on the present moment, and gain the clarity needed to tackle whatever life throws at you.

Sleep is a critical part of our overall health and well-being, yet it is often overlooked. Quality sleep not only allows us to recharge and reset mentally and physically but also helps to ensure that our bodies can cope with physical stressors such as illness or injury. Poor sleep quality can lead to dire consequences, including anxiety, depression, fatigue, poor concentration, and an increased risk of obesity. Therefore, it is so important to get adequate, restful sleep every night.

Sleep consists of two basic types: non-REM (non-rapid eye movement) and REM (rapid eye movement). Each type contains four stages, making up one sleep cycle. One night's worth of sleep can contain multiple cycles. Non-REM or quiet sleep occurs in the first three stages, while the fourth stage is REM.

The initial phase of sleep is a transition from wakefulness to non-rapid eye movement. This transition from wakefulness to sleep involves both mental and physical relaxation, as well as slowing down your heart rate, breathing, and body temperature. The second stage of sleep is light non-REM sleep. You will experience an increase in brain activity, as well as the production of sleep spindles. This stage is important for memory consolidation and retrieval. The third stage is deeper non-REM sleep, where your muscles become more relaxed, and your blood pressure and breathing rate slow down considerably. It is during this deep sleep that you are most likely to experience restful dreams. Finally, the fourth and last stage is REM sleep, also known as paradoxical sleep. Your body becomes almost completely immobilized while still being able to dream. This is where your eyes will move rapidly in various directions, and your brain activity increases to become more active. REM sleep plays a critical role in learning by helping you process and store memories from the day.

As a father, I am thankful that my son can get enough sleep each night. It is also amazing to think that animals like lions can sleep for so much of the day and still be so prolific in their royalty. However, it makes me wonder what my son and lions have in common that allows them to remain asleep for such prolonged periods. What I found in my research was that, like many of the animals on this planet, there is a universal order and structure to our sleep patterns.

When it comes to getting a good night's sleep, decluttering your mind is essential. Worrying about unnecessary things will lead to feelings of anxiety and stress that can disrupt your sleep. To help with this, make a list of the tasks you want to accomplish and focus on them instead of worrying over small matters. Keeping a notepad and pen nearby your bed is also a wonderful way to write down any anxious thoughts that come up during the night. Additionally, try to limit distractions from devices like phones or tablets if possible. These simple steps can help you drift off to sleep more easily and with less anxiety.

Exercise is a terrific way to help induce sleep. Even though you may want to sprint or lift weights, going for a light workout routine with some stretching can help your body go into rest mode. Pay attention to the timing and intensity of your workout as well. Additionally, it is best to avoid taking any form of a pre-workout supplement before exercising at night. These supplements may contain ingredients that may prevent anyone from dozing and therefore disrupt your sleep cycle.

When it comes to the amount of sleep we need, everyone is different. For example, an athlete may require more sleep than most people. Likewise, someone recovering from an injury or who is getting older may benefit from extra rest. Generally speaking, eight hours of sleep a night is sufficient. However, you do not need to keep a strict sleeping pattern. Allow yourself to be flexible by listening to your body and the amount of rest it needs.

Listen to your body

While pushing yourself to grow and reach new heights is important, it is also paramount to respect the limits of your body. Remember that true pain is often a sign that you should take a break, whereas discomfort can be an indication that you are pushing yourself beyond what you were previously capable of. Ultimately, it is up to you to decide if rest or training is the right decision. However, it is important to understand that your body needs to be respected and taken care of to reach your potential.

When it comes to the distinction between laziness and recovery, taking a break for restorative purposes is entirely permissible. If you have just completed a task or project that required tremendous effort and dedication, then there is nothing wrong with taking some time out of your day to recharge. Taking breaks can help maintain a healthy balance in our lives, helping us to stay productive without getting overwhelmed by the grind. On the other hand, laziness is when we avoid our responsibilities and neglect relationships that matter to us. Consequently, laziness is a sign of an imbalance in our lives.

Though I thought I was doing the right thing, overtraining can be one of the most damaging mistakes athletes make. It undermines the fundamental principles of rest and recovery upon which all successful training regimens are based. When you work out too intensely, too often, without allowing your body to recover between sessions, you risk burnout and injury. Overall, overtraining can lead to a decrease in performance and an increase in fatigue.

Fatigue is a state of mental and physical exhaustion that can have serious implications on athletic performance. It is important to recognize the symptoms of fatigue in order to take appropriate steps to address it. The first symptom of fatigue is often an inability to concentrate, which can lead to a decrease in reaction time, decision-making, and overall performance. Other physical signs include increased heart rate and breathing, loss of coordination, and intense muscle soreness. Mental symptoms can include feelings of frustration and difficulty focusing on the task at hand.

Breathing

I strongly advise you to incorporate breathing and meditation exercises into your recovery plan. Even if you only have the time or energy for 5 minutes of meditation each day, making this practice a regular part of your routine will yield significant positive results in the long term. Consistency is key when it comes to decreasing fatigue and preventing burnout.

As I studied more about the power of breath, I realized that it could be used as an effective tool to bring presence into the mind and body. With further research, I discovered the plethora of benefits associated with mindful breathing practices, such as reducing stress and anxiety, boosting energy levels, improving cognitive function, and enhancing overall mental clarity. I began to practice intentional breathing and was amazed by how much this simple act of awareness positively impacted my life.

In addition to intentional breathing, I also decided to engage in active meditation through sports such as rock climbing. This particular activity has taught me the importance of presence, as it requires focus and attention throughout each move. Additionally, the physical aspect of the sport provides an excellent and challenging workout that has helped me to stay fit and healthy.

When it comes to breathing, several types and styles depend on the situation. For example, when you are in a stressful or dangerous situation, your body will switch to survival-style breathing. This type of breathing is focused on getting as much oxygen into the system as possible so that you can escape whatever threat or peril you might be in. On the other hand, when you want to relax or practice mindfulness, there are different breathing techniques you can use. This could include abdominal breathing, diaphragm breathing, and chest breathing. All these methods help to achieve a relaxed state where your body can easily unwind.

Stress

Stress and anxiety are both emotions that can be triggered by life events. While they may seem similar, there is an important distinction between the two. Stress is a response to a stimulus or situation that causes emotional or physical tension. It can be caused by both positive and negative events. Anxiety, on the other hand, is an emotion characterized by feelings of fear, uneasiness, and worry. It is a stress reaction but can be caused by other events or situations as well. Stress is often interpreted as a feeling of pressure or urgency, while anxiety is more associated with dread and apprehension.

Understanding the difference between stress and anxiety can help you manage both emotions in better ways. Taking time to recognize the triggers for your stress and anxiety, as well as finding healthy outlets to reduce these feelings, can help you in leading a happier and healthier life. Understanding yourself and being able to identify when you are feeling stressed or anxious is a crucial step toward managing both emotions and living a productive life.

Getting enough rest and relaxation is an important part of living a healthy lifestyle. Taking time to relax can help reduce stress and anxiety, improve mood, lower blood pressure, provide relief from chronic pain, boost the immune system, and strengthen the cardiovascular system.

When trying to decrease stress, it is important to avoid any kind of mental stimulation. This means not doing anything that will require your brain to work hard and focus. Things like playing music or using screens can be stimulating for your mind and prevent you from truly recuperating.

Take a break from screens and devices. Switch it up and do something that relaxes your mind, like reading, stretching, or taking a warm bath. This will help you to get quality stress relief and have better rest at night. Spend time understanding what you need at any given moment. Whether it is a quick dopamine rush or some much-needed rest. If you feel the urge to spend time on screens, set a timer and limit yourself to only that much time.

On the other hand, if you need some rest, look for alternatives and refrain from going on your phone or laptop. Try out different techniques until you find something that helps to reduce your stress levels and gives you the rest you need.

Getting quality sleep is essential for managing stress. Poor sleeping habits, such as sleeping too little or too much, can worsen the effects of stress and make it even harder to bounce back from tough times. Inadequate sleep could affect your body's ability to regulate hormones responsible for controlling stress levels. This, in turn, leads to further physical and mental exhaustion. Symptoms such as chest pain, headaches, digestive issues, depression, anxiety, changes in sexual desire, appetite for food, and the inability to focus.

Stress can have an enormous impact on your eating habits and weight. While some people might respond by overeating, leading to an increase in weight, others may find that they do not eat much and can become underweight. In either case, the physical and psychological consequences can be damaging and should be avoided. Try waking up earlier and giving yourself a few extra minutes to prepare for the day. This will help you avoid the stress of being late due to having forgotten something or running into a problem at home. Additionally, arriving before you need to can give you time to relax, assess any potential problems ahead of time, and develop an idea of how long it will take to complete the task or arrive at your destination. Taking the time to plan and have a few extra minutes can significantly reduce stress throughout the day.

EPICDECA Journey

EPICDECA Story (Planning)

Mindset

The journey to self-discovery is never an easy one, as we are innately resistant to change. Our minds continuously search for ways to avoid any potential suffering, following the path of least resistance. This notion was challenged the year before the Epicdeca when I was hit by a careless truck driver while riding my bike at Ultraman Canada. This unfortunate incident provided me with a newfound perspective and a unique opportunity to confront these natural tendencies.

By pushing myself to my physical and mental limits, I discovered an inner strength and resilience that had been previously hidden from me. It showed me that the power of the mind is our most extreme and valuable asset and that when we focus our minds on something, we can reach achievements beyond our comprehension.

Despite being hit by a truck at Ultraman Canada, I was determined to finish the race. Regardless of my injuries, I stood back up, and my crew patched up anything that was not too serious. My handlebar had been broken, so they taped it together as best they could. After this unfortunate turn of events, I still had 200 km of cycling and a double marathon ahead of me, yet I was focused on continuing. I had trained and prepared for this race for months, and I was not going to let a truck derail me from completing it. I was going to finish Ultraman Canada, no matter what. My resilience and perseverance paid off as I eventually discovered new mental heights.

That experience taught me an invaluable lesson: that no matter how difficult the road ahead of me may seem, I have the power to rise and ride.

The thing about life is that it can sometimes seem like we are just going through the motions without ever making a real impact. These clouds of uncertainty and confusion seemed to linger for years, trapping me in an endless cycle of self-doubt. I knew that there had to be a way to free myself from this prison, but I could not see the solution. Then one day, it dawned on me that my mental blockage was helping me to find new clarity.

I realized that by taking a step back and reflecting on the life choices I had made before this point, I could start to understand my current situation. This newfound perspective allowed me to move forward and make more conscious decisions about how to approach the problem at hand. It was through this process that I learned an invaluable lesson: In order to overcome any obstacle, we must first learn to understand our minds. As I later discovered from my experience in Ironman racing, it is not the body or its endurance that determines success; it is the strength of the mind that makes all the difference. By taking control of my thoughts and emotions, I was able to push through whatever mental barriers were blocking my path and reach a new level of success.

It took me some time to realize that mental health is just as important as physical health. It was not until I began to understand the power of the mind and controlling how we think, feel, and behave that I began to realize this. My mind was highly distorted and clouded with thoughts that brought me down and made it difficult to take any meaningful action. So, I started to make a conscious effort to pay attention to my thoughts and emotions, to challenge them, and then replace them with more positive and empowering ones.

I knew I had to make a mindset shift if I wanted to succeed, and so I arbitrarily chose two variables that would outline a clear divide; hence I adopted the 80-20 rule. This rule states that 80% of the work for any goal should be allocated to mental preparation, and 20% should be devoted to physical preparation. Doing so would ensure I was focusing on the most significant variable.

Hunger mindset

The truth was that I felt powerless to change my circumstances, and I had no idea how to get out of

this depressive state of mind. But I had a deep burning desire to learn and grow and to become something more than what my current life was offering. I realized that the key to my recovery was understanding how our brain controls our body and behavior. I also had to learn more about the inner workings of my brain and how it affected my emotions. So, I decided to learn everything I could about the science of the mind and started researching neuroplasticity, cognitive behavior therapy, and metaphysic.

Teachable

Every opportunity became a challenge to build a stronger mindset. For instance, after starting my journey as an ultra-endurance athlete, I joined a local elite running club. These guys were running so fast that I could barely keep up. I would always finish last at every workout. This helped me reinforce a deep sense of humility which would eventually prove to be useful on this journey.

I read books about running and the mentality behind these spectacular humans. I remember watching a video of Eliud Kipchoge, who ran a marathon in under two hours. The video was meant to push the boundaries of what was humanely believed to be possible. He participated in a project that required him to run a little over 21 km/h for 2 hours. To put it into perspective, this is exactly how fast a normal human being would go on a joy ride with their bicycle.

One thing I noticed was how composed this phenomenal athlete was as compared to any other runner. It told me the man certainly had the body, natural skills, and strength to perform at an elite level. But most importantly, Eliud Kipchoge had the mindset to carry him through exhaustive times under pressure compared to other runners in his category.

Another impactful moment was a motivational video by David Goggins. This man retired from the navy seals and became an ultra-athlete and author, and he continues serving the world in multiple avenues. David stated that when you want to resign, you still have 40% left in the tank. He used a tank or basin as a metaphor to create a bridge, referring to a location to deposit and withdraw our energy from. These nuggets of information were then stored in my brain and used like tiny pieces of armor that protected me from the thoughts of giving up in difficult moments.

Attitude

To be successful in life, I had to learn how to develop a good attitude and approach each situation with a positive mindset. This meant changing the way I think and how I deal with adversity. It was difficult to keep a good attitude when so much negativity surrounded me, but I kept reminding myself that my attitude was a choice.

During my entire lifetime, I experienced rejection and loneliness regularly. This would be a constant ordeal, and I had to figure out what was wrong. I eventually came to understand that there was a difference between having physical talent and emotional maturity. While some of my competitors had the natural ability to run fast, they were often lacking in other areas.

This lesson was brought home to me one weekend when some of the best runners from the area were participating in a half marathon. Despite being outmatched physically, I decided to join them on the run. At the end of the race, one of these elite athletes finished in second place out of over a thousand competitors.

I was filled with admiration for this runner and decided to reach out to congratulate him. But he never acknowledged my message, not even with a simple reply. It was then that I understood the importance of emotional development and how it cannot be substituted for natural talent.

It was after this experience that I developed an attitude of resilience. I realized that the only way to be successful was to remain positive even in the face of rejection. By understanding that some people will never acknowledge our efforts, we learn to persevere and take joy in the accomplishments that are within our reach.

Decision Making

When I heard about Epic5, I realized that there was a level of endurance beyond the Ultraman. Epic5 is a challenge of immense proportions, requiring athletes to complete five full Ironman triathlons in 5 days on 5 Hawaiian Islands. It is a feat of physical and mental stamina that few can imagine. It takes an extraordinary individual to even consider such a challenge, let alone complete it.

Chad Bentley is one of those extraordinary humans. After he and I completed Ultraman Canada, I noticed him talking about it as one of the biggest challenges he had ever faced. Seeing his dedication to the event, I knew that I wanted to know more and gain a better understanding of what Epic5 was all about.

I asked Chad a lot of questions, and he was more than happy to answer them. He told me all the details about Epic5 and how he managed to complete it. He also shared some of his amazing experiences during the challenge, which made me even more excited about the idea of taking on this challenge.

EPICDECA STORY (PLANNING)

Wishing that one day I would compete in comparable events, I went on my way to complete different endurance races. During one of those trips, I overheard someone mention they were registered as an Epicdeca athlete. I was told all the details of this unique competition. Due to the logistical demands of the event, the race director was only able to open the registration for ten athletes worldwide. This was a level of fitness that I felt was unattainable and seemed like something out of a dream.

Simultaneously, while I was in other races, one of the ten registered athletes of Epicdeca, named Joe Jaffe, went to do a race in Florida. Joe was an athlete I used to follow on social media as one of the legends of the sport of ultra-triathlon. During this Florida cycling competition, an inattentive driver struck Joe. The vehicle went away without ever stopping, and Joe was left with wounds to recover from. At the beginning of February, Joe posted on his social media that he would have to drop out from the start list of the Epicdeca.

I contacted him to wish him well. As we chatted, we discussed that he would not be able to recover the hefty sum of money he had put down for the event registration. I asked him if I could purchase his registration. He franticly laughed as he knew that this deca-triathlon was starting in less than 90 days and was the most extreme adventure triathlon that was ever created. Nonetheless, he asked the main organizer if transferring his registration was within the realm of possibilities. Within a few days, the organizer agreed under the condition I would go through a screening interview process.

Before even committing to do the race, I needed to make sure I had a crew of at least four people to follow me. I was somehow under the impression that this would be viewed as a vacation for most. The draft package I offered included flights, food, hotel, and transportation to all the Hawaiian Islands for 15 days in the month of May. I messaged many of my contacts, and even though the deal seemed as appealing as it could be, many rejected the offer.

One of them was my father. Although he would have surely come if he could, my father also knew he would not be able to help me as he never took part in crewing in such a gigantic event. His helpful tip for choosing a team was to select individuals who had already been through something similar in nature.

I contacted my coach to ask for his opinion on whether I should take on the Epicdeca race. He said that it was not a good idea this year and that it would be wise to postpone it. He was aware I was on a destructive path, and his advice was not intended to lead me down further. He said that the decision was mine and mine alone. So, I took his advice but decided to continue my path. I knew that if I could put together a suitable team, then I could do the Epicdeca. I started by evaluating my physical and mental capabilities, then looked for compatible athletes who had a similar mindset and commitment as I did.

I contacted Shane Mascarin, whom I raced with at Ultraman Canada the year prior. He was an ultra-athlete, and I recall how this guy completed Ultraman Canada while undergoing shoulder surgery only six months prior. I knew that if there was anyone strong enough mentally to help me finish this event, it would be him. For Shane, this opportunity was an easy decision. Shane spoke to his wife, Sara, and they accepted within a day. In fact, Sara crewed for most of his events, which proved her resilience to support these endeavors.

Michelle Bukowski, who is a nurse and an accomplished ultra-athlete, was originally scheduled to crew for Joe Jaffe. She kindly agreed to join forces with us and bring over all the organization she had completed in the last two years. Lastly, another crew member, who will be named Billy for confidentiality reasons, accepted the offer.

When I decided to take on the challenge of Epicdeca, there was no going back. I felt a sense of motivation and purpose that I had not experienced in a while. The adventure ahead was daunting, but the rewards seemed worth it. I committed to the challenge wholeheartedly, understanding that this was a journey of self-discovery and growth.

During the preliminary planning, we projected to separate the team into two even groups. This would ease the rotation schedule to have two people with the athlete while a minimum of two would rest.

Sara and Michelle were appointed as the leaders of their respective squads, and Michelle was the overall crew chief. Basically, the person who would be responsible for making any decisions in my absence of judgment.

The day Michelle accepted to be the crew chief, I rushed to the bank to complete the money transfer for Joe. On my way, Joe called me to send him only half the previously agreed amount. I was overwhelmed by this gift to support my endeavors. During the interview process, I spoke to the main organizer. I was able to demonstrate my commitment and enthusiasm for the event. I highlighted that while I may be new to this race style, I have considerable experience in long-distance triathlon. I showed that I was confident in my abilities but also willing to learn and grow.

That evening, I wanted to celebrate my confirmation as a registered athlete. I decided the best way to do that was to run ten kilometers. I took my son for the ride, and he was delighted to sit in a sled while I pulled him along. He squealed with laughter as the snow flew around us, and I felt such immense joy at the moment. We ran together, and I experienced a feeling of accomplishment that was indescribable. This was just another reminder of why I decided to pursue my dreams and never give up on life. Once the crew was assembled, I came to the next part of preparation. Any event's financial aspect should also be considered, which is why I contacted my bank. I knew I was ready to go into financial difficulties if it meant doing this event. The bank only gave me advice because they knew, in the end, it was my money, and I could do whatever I pleased with it. I was delighted they gave me the support I needed. The last part of the preparation was given access to my credit cards to Michelle and Sara. It was not an easy task; I had to trust two strangers with my financials, but this was a necessary step. I knew that if it were not for them, the event would not be successful.

Hire a Coach

Picture my coach's face when I talked to him about inserting the Epicdeca only two months before the event. My coach was speechless at first. Once he understood that this event would never happen again, he adopted the mentality of *"How can we make this happen"* which was essential to achieving my goals. After a brainstorming session together, we concluded that it was best to use the following two Ironman that was on the schedule as a training platform to test abilities and gear.

My coach was confident in his ability to train me. Despite his expertise and fantastic job providing impressive results, he knew he would have to direct me to another person when I approached him with this challenge. I already had a packed racing schedule with at least six other Ironman, including world championship races. Yet I still endeavored to complete the Epicdeca. He encouraged me to reconsider partaking in this affair. Even so, choosing to compete was one of the best decisions of my life.

Coach Jeff even directed me to get advice from Rich Roll. For those who are not familiar, Jason Lester and Rich Roll are true pioneers in the endurance sports world. After creating and completing the original Epic5 challenge, they demonstrated to thousands of athletes around the world that it was possible to achieve the seemingly impossible.

Although they no longer oversee the Epic5 franchise, their accomplishments provide a source of inspiration and motivation for others to attempt their versions of this ultra-endurance challenge. Unfortunately, my attempts to contact Rich Roll went unanswered, but the legacy of Jason and Rich remains in endurance sports as one of the greatest triumphs.

My decision to attempt a double version of the Epic5 challenge was motivated by both admirations for Jason, Rich, Chad, and Joe, as well as a desire to prove to myself that I can break through limits set by my doubt. In my application to Epicdeca, I expressed a desire to meet Rich Roll.

It was my assessment that he would be an excellent example of someone who had taken ownership of their life and forged a path of success. He overcame a challenging lifestyle and has since become an influential speaker and author. Rich Roll is now a role model and an inspiration to many who are seeking to make changes in their lives.

Strategize

Having decided to partake in the Epicdeca, I knew that it was time to take the necessary steps to make the event a success. To do so, I formulated a 16-page plan that outlined the details of my decision. This plan included general ideas about the types of mental emergencies I might face during the event, such as what signs and symptoms should be looked out for.

It also included specific notions like the pressure tires and how much salt I would require in an hour of exercise based on various levels of temperature that could be expected in the Hawaiian archipelago. In other words, I had taken the time to prepare for most eventualities and was now ready to take on the next part of preparation.

Having carefully put together a plan, I was ready to present it to the crew. With team members from different states in the US, and provinces in Canada, we discussed the plan as a team and built on everyone's input through online calls. We all agreed that it was a comprehensive plan, and with this agreement came a sense of eagerness to take on the challenge. We discussed our roles, the logistics involved in getting to Hawaii, and the training we would need to undergo in the months leading up to the event.

At this point, my crew chief asked me a question: Was I going to race, or was I merely looking for ways to finish the event? I answered that I wanted to finish it and did not consider the event a race. I could see how stunned she was by the response. I placed the event and my will to complete it in a category of challenges instead of competitions. This critical decision decreased all other expectations and results for my crew's mind and mine.

Value System

In the northern parts of Quebec, there was no one to rely on for help. My father was usually spending months in Florida with his wife. Additionally, most of my family had already moved away from this region. I knew that in order to be successful as a single father, I had to make my relationship with my son a priority. Therefore, I dedicated my energy and time to ensure that I provided him with the care and guidance he needed to grow into a healthy, well-adjusted individual.

I did so by reading books and completing exercises that would improve my parenting skills. The book, "The Love Dare for Parents," was a wonderful way of reinforcing the importance of our relationship and promoting gratitude. One of the dares from the book was for me to post a list on the fridge. This list contained things that I was thankful for, such as spending time with my son and telling him that I loved him "today." This simple act was a powerful reminder to my son. Seeing those words of love and appreciation helped him solidify my priorities and commitment to him.

Throughout the process of parenting my son, I realized that nothing was more important than fostering a strong and meaningful relationship with him. I learned to create certain rituals, such as spending quality time together or engaging in regular conversations so that he would be able to connect and express himself. This allowed us to form a secure bond that has only grown stronger over the years. With that in mind, I had to find a way to train for the triathlon without relying solely on physical activity. I needed to find an occupation that felt fun and engaging for my son and something he could look forward to. I realized that the winter season was the perfect time to practice skiing with him. It was something that would require me to be out in the cold and build up my endurance while simultaneously bonding with him.

In the beginning, it was quite a challenge, but as my son quickly picked up the sport, he began to enjoy it even more than I did. Taking the time to engage in this activity with him provided us both with a sense of accomplishment and joy. Something we both desperately needed while going through the healing process.

Through this experience, I learned that sometimes, the best way to recover from an illness is not just through physical activity. Sometimes, it is a recipe for both physical and mental practices. Skiing with my son provided this perfect combination.

Mind Games

Although I was faced with a serious dearth of resources and even lacked the training for the Epicdeca, I was determined to not let this stop me. This lack of resources was mainly due to my location in the northern part of Quebec, where snow covers the ground for most of the year, making it a difficult environment to perform triathlon disciplines. But I was resolute in my ambition and decided to use this adversity as a source of inspiration rather than defeat.

Having my son full-time meant that I had to prioritize his needs, which, unfortunately, meant not going to the pool. Despite the less-than-ideal circumstances, I was determined to keep up my swimming training. So, I adapted by changing the height of my ski poles to mimic the same swimming motions. Doing so enabled me to simulate the same muscles I would use for swimming. This meant that despite not having access to a pool, I was still able to maintain my physical conditioning. It was a creative solution that further reinforced the importance of setting priorities. By prioritizing my son and being available to have fun together, I was still able to achieve my fitness goals.

For cycling, I used an electric trainer in the living room at my dad's house while watching through the window unbelievable amounts of snowfall. The roads covered in snow and ice were never an option for riding my triathlon bike outside.

For running, I would run on the snow under brutally cold temperatures. I had built a harness for running and attached it to a sled with a couple of mountain-climbing carabiners. When the roads were flat, I would run with the sled attached to the harness while my son enjoyed being pulled in the chariot. He loved it, and so did I, for it felt like a powerful display of strength and courage. We would be out there in all kinds of weather, no matter the wind chill or temperature. This was my way of building resilience, as I found that running in difficult conditions made me a tougher person. Despite the cold, it felt incredible to be outside and push myself to the limits. In this way, I was able to develop a powerful sense of perseverance that carried over to Epicdeca.

I found that these expeditions with my son were a fantastic way to build physical endurance as well as mental resilience. We would end up climbing mountains together and reaching new heights. Even when the terrain would not flat, my son and I were determined to brave the cold hills. We climbed mountains together, overcoming seemingly insurmountable obstacles for a small child. I was able to challenge us both and push our limits while still having the safety of knowing that I had a sled if he needed to rest.

It was a terrific way to teach my son the value of perseverance and hard work while still having an exciting time in nature together. The beauty of the snow-covered mountains was an incredible sight, and it was worth every step. With the proper gear, such as snowshoes, we were able to make the most out of our adventure.Despite the fun activities that I took part in, my mental health still was not at its best. However, by setting daily reminders for myself to continue, such as in the process of the *Rule of 3*, and constantly visualizing my goal of completing the Epicdeca and other triathlons, I was able to keep pushing forward. The 'Rule of 3' really helped me focus on making minor changes each day, which accumulated over time and eventually enabled me to reach larger objectives.

I had to learn to push myself past my comfort zone, and this often meant engaging in some serious mind games. I discovered that there was power in challenging myself and pushing my limits, no matter how uncomfortable it felt. It was through this process of trial and error that I slowly began to become the best version of myself. I have since come to understand that if you want to create a better life for yourself, then sometimes you need to take the initiative and be willing to change your old habits.

EPICDECA Story (Strategy)

Environment

I eventually resolved to teach myself the skills I needed to change my circumstances. It was a difficult journey learning how to take control of my environment and my mental state, but I was determined to find success. My efforts paid off, and I soon saw the same mindset of perseverance spreading in my son, who went on to become part of the ski team.

One of the most fascinating aspects of parenting is watching the ripple effect it has on others. We often do not realize how our actions and values shape the lives of others, and it is sometimes only when we see our children interacting with their peers that we understand the true reach of our influence. Recently I was reminded of this when my son told me that his friends on the ski team were surprised to hear him say that his dad pulls him up the mountain in a sled. It was then that I realized how unique our parenting style must have seemed to them, even though to my son, all of this seemed normal.

I am thankful to have realized on time that although all parents enjoyed watching their kids ski, I needed to provide myself with a community of like-

minded individuals who would practice triathlon. We were lucky to have been surrounded by competent people who could help enhance my son's skiing skills. However, it was not only by focusing on the physical and mental aspects of training that I could prepare and do well for Epicdeca. Along with running on snow and adjusting my ski pole height, I had to also set realistic goals and change my environment.

I also learned throughout my many travels to consider the environment to live in, both in terms of its location and its community. I acquired this knowledge the year before when traveling to Mexico for UltraMX515. I was initially skeptical as I had been warned against visiting the area due to its perceived dangers. To my surprise, this region was also home to some of the kindest individuals I had ever met. The local people were incredibly welcoming, and the environment was filled with a genuine sense of community.

This experience demonstrated to me the importance of the community and environment when considering a place to live. This case taught me that it is essential to be aware of both the positive aspects and potential risks associated with any location. Additionally, it is important to understand that the people in a community can have an enormous influence on one's overall experience of the place and their sense of well-being.

However, in this case, I needed both the location and a triathlon community to grow toward the goal of completing the Epicdeca successfully.

To make a successful change to my environment, I had to prepare properly. This meant researching the best ways to approach my desired change, identifying any potential risks or challenges, and creating a clear plan of action for how I wanted to move forward. By taking the time to carefully plan the details of my change of environment, I was able to ensure that it was done in an organized and effective manner.

Planning

When I graduated with an engineering degree, I did not think I would be using it in a way that was so different from what I envisioned. Little did I know the design process I learned in my degree would be so useful in planning and organizing an event like the Epicdeca triathlon. From understanding how to create a plan, develop a prototype, and continually improve and iterate on the design until it was complete, I discovered that my degree was more valuable than I ever imagined. This experience has taught me a great deal about how to apply my education in real-world situations and to be creative and innovative in thinking about how to utilize the knowledge I gained.

EPICDECA STORY (STRATEGY)

I knew that knowledge acquisition was one of the primary pillars when it came to planning any project. It was essential to understand the existing best practices and take advice from those who had already completed similar projects. Thus, I sought out experts in the field who could provide me with invaluable advice and resources. Because this feat had never been done before, I was not able to rely on anyone to provide me with a clear road map. Even so, I took the initiative to reach out for help by calling people who had comparable experiences. Joe Jaffe had already completed the Epic5 a few years back. For that reason, he was an obvious first choice to acquire knowledge. We had a long online meeting to know the details of Epicdeca. During the call, he confirmed the famous tales of his nutrition being true. The man would feed his body with gas station pizza and fast-food burgers. It was by far the most extreme fueling strategy I had ever heard as an ultra-athlete.

I could not even imagine sending my crew to a local fast-food restaurant to get junk food and referring to such behavior as energizing. Because I lacked an ideal training setting, I compensated with a diet that was much cleaner and rich in nutrients. Joe's wisdom was invaluable in my preparation for the race. He advised me to make sure I took care of my crew, even if it meant sacrificing time on the course. I learned that when the conditions got tough, prioritizing comfort over speed was the best way to ensure a successful outcome. Joe also shared a story about his experience racing in the event. He recounted how during one of the legs, a huge storm hit, and all the athletes ended up having to ride their bikes through water that was half the height of their wheels. Despite the challenge, he managed to finish and imparted his wisdom to me that day.

Chad Bentley was another ultra-athlete whom I had the privilege of learning. He shared his knowledge about Epic5, and one of his stories particularly resonated with me. On day five of the race, he was exhausted and had to take a quick nap in the crew vehicle. He recalled the sleep he got being deep and one of the best he had ever experienced in his life. Hearing Chad's story made me even more aware of the difficulty of this race and how it was even more extreme than I had anticipated. He showed me that taking care of my physical rest was just as important as putting in the miles on the course.

Support

The best thing that happened to me was that a few people believed in me. I was disappointed to discover it was not the people I thought would be there for me in the first place who would eventually offer the most assistance. Regardless, I appreciate that those random, sporadically met strangers believed that I could succeed and invested in this process.

Pierre-Marc, the owner of Velocite Concept, a local bike shop, was one of those people. He noticed my hard work, dedication, and resilience. He could have just passed me by, but instead, he offered to provide me with a discount on my bike parts and accessories.

It was surprising to me because he was not going to get anything out of this deal like a fast athlete or podium. Nevertheless, he also knew that I was not going to give up at the slightest obstacle I would inevitably have to face. These rebates were often just a few dollars here or there for him, but for me, they made all the difference. It gave me the belief that I could make it, and suddenly, I had a renewed sense of purpose.

I was happy that Joe Jaffe and Velo-Cite only gave me a discount on what I needed and did not give me their goods for free. This forced me to be hungry and get the rest of the money if I wanted to be part of this challenge. I had heard of so many athlete stories who got "free rides" to all the best the world has to offer and yet would not appreciate their opportunity. Although phenomenal athletes, they would go on and waste all their lottery winnings by not being hungry.

With a clear understanding of what I needed to do and the people who would help me, I set out to acquire the necessary tools for the job.

After consulting with Joe and Pierre-Marc, I decided to buy a cheap bike for the cycling portion of the Epicdeca. It was a sensible choice as some race bikes can cost more than a sports car. Because comfort was discussed as a principal factor when cycling long distances, going with a road bike over a triathlon bike seemed like an intelligent decision. I also decided against disc brakes as they are known to bend when traveling. With all this in mind, I purchased a cheap old road bike from an online trading site that I brought to Velocite to get fitted and upgrade some parts.

When it came to spare parts, I knew that I had to be prepared. Going on an adventure of such a scale could come with many surprises, including the need for spare parts. I had to think about anything that potentially broke during this challenge. This is because there are only bike shops on the first two islands, and once we were on the other islands, I would not be able to go to a bike shop for any spare parts. I took several tires, tubes, and even a derailleur hanger. The last part may seem excessive, but you can never predict what can happen in the middle of a race. I also had to think about the nighttime rides, the rain, and the potential cold temperatures that could drop during the night close to 13°C. I had to make sure I had the right equipment to tackle the race with confidence while traversing the roads of the islands at night. To this end, I purchased lamps, rain jackets, gloves, and even a rain cover for my helmet. I did not know what was awaiting me on the other side and did not want to be unprepared. I remember thinking to myself, "better safe than sorry," when packing my gear before the Epicdeca.

At the same time, ensuring that my safety was not compromised and placed as a priority. I knew that spending more on quality parts like a good bib and quality jerseys was an investment worth making as it would prevent bigger injuries and be safer. Pierre-Marc also suggested getting some flashy jerseys to help with safety while cycling. So, I got some bright jerseys which I thought was a great idea.

Accountability

My son was my top priority, and I wanted to make sure he was taken care of while I participated in the Epicdeca. His mother and I agreed that it would be best for him to stay with her in Canada during the event, as this was not an appropriate environment for a child.

I kissed my son goodbye and set off to Texas to put my plan and equipment to the test. I was both excited and nervous, but I knew that this journey was necessary. I had put a lot of thought into my plan and the equipment, so now it was time to see if it would hold up. I was also excited to explore the unknown and evaluate my mettle in an unfamiliar environment.

When I first arrived in Galveston, Texas, I knew that my body would need to become acclimatized to the warmer climate. Having come from a snow-filled mountain environment to one of the hot beaches and temperatures reaching 30°C, I knew that some acclimatization was in order. With this in mind, it was amusing that I would have to incorporate tanning sessions and training under the sun into my workout routine.

I planned to ride my road bike for the Ironman 70.3 in Galveston, as this would be a wonderful way to test my new equipment. As I was unpacking my bags, I realized that I had forgotten my wetsuit. This was a critical piece of equipment for this event, so I rushed to the Ironman tent and asked about purchasing one. Fortunately, the woman at the tent had one in my size, and unfortunately, it was the most expensive wetsuit on offer.

Despite its hefty price tag, I knew that it was necessary to get the job done, so I made the purchase. I am glad to say that in the end, it was a great purchase, as I comfortably completed the half

Ironman wearing my new wetsuit. The back support it provided gave me additional comfort, and I was confident the wetsuit would hold up even in the most difficult of conditions.

Upon completing the half Ironman in Galveston, I decided to move to Woodlands, Texas. My stay at the Crowne Plaza allowed me to meet the whole staff, get to know them, and build relationships. The hotel provided the perfect environment for me to prepare for the Epicdeca journey coming ahead. It was an investment in my health, and I knew it would be worthwhile. The staff was incredibly friendly, helpful, and encouraging, which was a great boost for me.

I had to be resourceful and approach this challenge from a different angle than climbing mountains, so I started looking for swimming coaches in Woodlands. Sure enough, I was able to find a few willing to help me out. Tim Floyd was well-known and respected in the triathlon community, having already coached professional athletes for years. The next month was intense. I was pushing myself every day in the pool with Tim as my coach. I knew that he would be able to help me refine my technique, build up my endurance, and keep me accountable toward my target event. I kept Jeff as my triathlon coach in Canada because he would organize my overall schedule, while Tim took care of the swimming component. This allowed me to focus on honing my skills and pushing myself in the pool while still having a plan for the rest of my training.

With their help and a lot of hard work on my part, I was able to develop the technique and endurance needed to feel confident in the water in preparation for the Epicdeca. After accepting Tim's invitation to his private facility, I arrived with high hopes of improving my technique through video analysis. By studying the videos and Tim's expert advice, I was able to gain a deeper understanding of my movements and how to improve them. With every drill and every practice session, I could feel my technique becoming sharper and more precise. With Tim's guidance, my confidence in my technique soared, and I knew I was headed for success.

Although I was dealing with the pain of tendinitis on my left foot, by the grace of Tim's friend, who happened to be the owner of a Texas Running Store, I was blessed with a pair of sandals to help me out. Not only did they provide relief from the pain, but they also allowed me to continue my journey with more confidence and peace of mind. It was an unforgettable experience to witness the power of community, and this small gesture of kindness reminded me that we all need each other to succeed.

I was determined to see if the sandals reduced the pain enough to be able to run. I also needed to assess running shoes, so I registered for a half marathon. This was an excellent way to test the efficacy of the shoes in sustaining pain in a running context.

Cheering

Meanwhile, I quickly realized that cycling was more than just a leisurely activity to do in my dad's living room. It was also a way for me to challenge myself and push my boundaries. I was constantly striving to get better, faster, and stronger as I joined a group on their weekly rides. Every time I thought I had reached my limit, the group pushed me further, encouraging me to reach for more.

The feeling of exhilaration I experienced from cycling with such a large group of experienced people was something that stuck with me. The danger of being so close to other riders at such a fast speed was something that I faced and embraced head-on. The experience of feeling the wind rush past me and the people bumping into me made it an unforgettable experience. Cycling taught me to take risks, push my limits, and be mindful of my surroundings. In the end, it was a thrilling way to evaluate my mettle and see what I am capable of.

The training was a delicate balance between pushing to my limits and resting. I found it humorous that while the former was a necessity, the latter was done in the form of sun tanning. It was important to keep my skin healthy and protected, so I took a few moments each day to do what I needed to be safe in the sun. It was a strange yet satisfying experience and a reminder that I was taking the necessary steps to ensure my body could safely do the Epicdeca.

I had worked hard in the weeks before to build a network of people who would be there to support me when I competed in my second Ironman of the month. As I faced the challenge of an endurance race that was long and grueling, I knew my friends would be there to keep encouraging me. It was a true testament to the power of community and the strength that comes from shared experience.

I was determined to prove that I could push myself and make it through Epicdeca. My drive to succeed was strong, and I was willing to do whatever it took to make sure that I would finish. The final test was Ironman Woodlands in Texas. Despite having to push my body to the extreme, such as not sleeping the night before to mimic the mental fatigue in the Epicdeca, it was all worth it in the end. I had set a goal of completing this Ironman in 12 hours, and I had done it.

Similar Languages

That sense of loneliness was still lingering in my mind, no matter where I went. It felt like I was isolated in a strange world that I could never understand. Even when surrounded by a multitude of people, I felt disconnected from them, as if we were from different planets. That feeling was endlessly haunting me whether I went skiing in Quebec or swimming in Texas. In those moments, I could not find a sense of belonging, no matter how hard I tried. Despite engaging in activities that were shared, I felt incredibly alone.

It was an immensely disconcerting feeling and something I wanted desperately to overcome. Eventually, I did, by understanding that my sense of belonging did not have to come from the people around me. Rather, it was something I had to create within myself. It was only then that I began to gain a sense of confidence and self-understanding, realizing that I could be content in any situation.

It was not easy, but it was worth it. I realized that being diverse is something to be embraced, not shied away from. I learned that even if some people do not appreciate my presence, there will always be those who do, and that is what truly matters. I am now able to look at any situation with a sense of optimism and joy, knowing that I can find my sense of belonging if I look within. My journey of self-discovery has taught me to appreciate and accept differences, even if others cannot. In a way, it has become my superpower.

I had to come to understand that we are all on a journey of self-discovery, and no matter how hard it can be, it is essential to our growth. It might not be the people you expect who will help you out of it, but if you look closer, you will find those who will understand and appreciate you for a short while. We all face different struggles, but we are not alone in our journey and can learn from each other's stories and experiences. Understanding this helped me let go of my loneliness and find a sense of belonging in the world around me. I learned many life lessons along my journey that helped to prepare me, and I was ready to take on the next challenge.

Community Expectations

So, a couple of days after completing Ironman Woodlands, I jumped on a plane to the island of Oahu in Hawaii. I decided to show up two weeks before the challenge to familiarize myself with the terrain, explore the community, and let my body acclimate to the hot and humid environment. Turns out, it was an excellent decision regarding the event. After arriving in Hawaii, I followed the same process that previously gave the best results. I set up my gear in the hotel room, then I contacted the area's cycling, swimming, and running communities. Only two people replied, and so I was set to learn from these new friends. Besides, I kept doing the workouts that my coach assigned. Getting out of my comfort zone and meeting strangers was challenging, but I pushed myself.

One of the things I discovered about Hawaii is that it has some interesting weather patterns. For example, I remember one time when I had planned a long bike ride, and when I looked outside, it was raining. Even though everyone else was wearing shorts and sandals, I decided to take the opportunity to try out my rain gear. By the time I made it downstairs, the rain had stopped! The rain was short-lived, and quickly the sun came out again. This is because Hawaii has a tropical weather system where rain appears in short bursts but does not hang around for long. Only when a storm is especially strong will Hawaii experience more significant rain periods. Another thing I learned about the climate of Hawaii is that it is ridiculously hot, so the rain does not usually linger on your body for long.

During those two weeks, my body had time to adjust to the environment and the climate. I also met a few key people, like the bike mechanic of the event. He took me on a scenic bike tour of the island to explore how people drive and what terrain I would encounter during the event. After exploring Oahu on my own, I decided to take a plunge and snorkel with sharks without the protection of a cage. It was an incredible experience that pushed my boundaries and reinforced my confidence when it came to swimming in the ocean. The crew on the expedition was also a major help, giving us tips and teaching us about the behavior of these large carnivorous creatures. They taught us to remain calm and not to move around too much, as that could appear threatening to the sharks. We were also told to keep direct eye contact with the sharks. In short, we were taught to respect their space and stay vigilant of our environment.

One of the best things about visiting Oahu was discovering all the delicious acai places. Not only were these places great for fruits and shakes, but they also offered a wide variety of dishes that made it easy to find something I liked. Furthermore, the acai places were often located in pleasant outdoor settings, which made them beautiful places to relax and enjoy some delicious food. In addition to providing tasty food, Oahu's acai places allowed me to meet some of the locals and learn more about their culture. Furthermore, they provided a fantastic way to get energized before and after my workouts.

Then came a moment of realization on my trip to this beautiful island of Hawaii that made me understand the need for mental health work. On the island's west side, I saw a heartbreaking sight that would be a challenge for the strongest of us to ignore. Miles of homeless individuals lived in tents, with only tarps as a roof over their heads. I had conversations with the locals and found out that most of these people were facing mental health issues. That made me realize how important it is to work on addressing mental health topics. It reinforced my desire to complete the event I had planned for this trip. After all, I was one of the guys who was, just a few months before that point, laying on a couch looking at a ceiling and in the worst state of mental health. Seeing the condition of others drove me to action and reinforced the reason I needed to finish this event. I had an understanding that mental health is not something to be taken lightly, and I chose to be outspoken about it.

A couple of days before the journey, all the crew members arrived. Although it was the first time we had ever met in person or spent any length of time together as a team, the crew chief quickly took charge and confirmed that we had all the necessary supplies to make our journey a success. We quickly got acquainted, and the camaraderie was palpable.

The next morning, we set off on our island tour with a sense of purpose and excitement. We visited some of the most beautiful natural locations on the island, taking time to admire its majesty while still being mindful of the task at hand. As the sun began to set, we stopped for a team photo. Despite our vastly diverse backgrounds and perspectives, there was an unmistakable bond between us. We were unified in our mission, and I felt a newfound sense of camaraderie as we watched the sunset together from our hotel pool area.

Day 1: Oahu Island

This was the moment I had been preparing for. After months of challenging work, my plans and preparations had culminated at this very moment. I was about to face a challenge that could make or break me. I knew I had done my best, and now it was time for me to go all over Hawaii to evaluate this plan.

The first two iron distances were on the island of Oahu. Here, I learned the difference between an Ironman and an iron-distance. The main difference is that an Ironman is a branded event with thousands of people competing, with the ultimate goal of having as many complete it as possible.

However, the Epicdeca brings all the challenges of an Ironman in a much more hazardous setting. Without any traffic control, athletes must be aware of their surroundings and pay attention to the terrain. To make Epicdeca even more challenging, there are no dedicated washrooms. The athletes must find alternative solutions to their restroom needs, and all this must be factored into their plan. Due to island hopping, the athletes must also be prepared for unexpected variables that could alter their plans.

Additionally, the athletes were certainly put to the test with the limited luggage allowance on the tiny planes. With only two checked-in bags and one bike box, athletes had to carefully consider what was essential for a successful race on these islands. It is this sense of adventure, uncertainty, and danger that made the Epicdeca such an amazing challenge. We had to be prepared to face whatever came our way and take it in stride.

Normally a triathlon includes a swim, bike, then run, in this specific order. The sport comprises two transitions in the middle of each discipline. The first transition often referred to as T1, is between the swim and the bike. The second transition, or T2, is conducted between the bike and run. This order of swim, T1, bike, T2, and run can be altered during multiday Ultra-triathlons, including the Epicdeca.

The organizers understood that when participating in such a challenge, we may encounter unexpected issues, such as the unfortunate situation of having our luggage arrive later than expected. They had made provisions for this and were open to modifying the predetermined order of each discipline in an emergency. So, if our bike did not arrive at the same time as the athlete, we could still do the swim and the run, then switch up to the bike once it arrived. We just had to make sure we informed the organizers about any changes in advance. The rules of the game were strict and specific, with no exceptions. All athletes had to start with the same discipline and be on the starting line at the same time. If for any reason, an alternative plan was necessary, officials would adjust the disciplines accordingly. The only requirement was that the full distance had to be completed. It was the job of the assigned officials to ensure that each athlete competed on a fair and level playing field, and their presence served to guarantee that the rules were conducted properly.

As the first day approached, we had a mixture of anxiety and excitement. We were all unfamiliar with each other's strengths and weaknesses but knew that it was essential to collaborate to finish the course. We needed to find ways of pacifying our fears while staying focused on the task ahead. We knew that any mistakes we made would have a ripple effect on the entire team, so each of us had to be disciplined and careful in our actions.

Despite the fact that we had ten athletes signed up for the race, only six of us reached the starting line. This was a disappointment to the race organizer, but all of us who were still participating agreed to proceed with the original plan. For some reason that is still unknown to everyone, the organizer arranged the first and second days in the unusual order of run, swim, and bike.

That first morning of the race, I was filled with a sense of anticipation. The sun had yet to rise, and the competition had begun, but there was something special in the air. I knew that this would be a race unlike any other I had done before, not just because of the location or the distance but also because of the people. I was surrounded by a group of talented and determined individuals, all of whom were striving to do their best.

The run that day went as expected — my legs were feeling a bit heavy from all the training and races I had done in Texas only weeks before. Even so, I felt a sense of invigorating energy as I embraced the challenge that lay ahead. The miles were passing quickly, and I could feel my body adjust to the terrain as I continued my journey. During the run, it was clear that some people were already struggling to adjust to it. However, one person made the situation even more difficult by displaying dangerous behaviors. The photographer hired for the event was taking pictures while standing on the road, dangerously blocking the athletes from running at their pace. I was not about to let this event go sideways because of a careless individual. At the same time, I also wanted to remain respectful and professional, so I warned the crew chief, Michelle, to communicate with the organizers. This way, they could warn him to be more mindful of where he was standing and take photos from a safe distance. Thankfully, we all managed to avoid any drama and finish the run portion of the first day in the parking lot, where the rest of the crew were waiting for their athletes.

I was incredibly grateful for Sara, who volunteered to be the support for every instance a paddler was required. No one argued as she was so animated to do so. She had vast knowledge of the equipment and much-needed experience. We were then able to take in the sights, which included some beautiful sea turtles that had made their way into the bay area. Even with the warm water, I opted to wear a wetsuit for extra buoyancy. This proved to be beneficial and allowed me to really get the most out of the experience.

Regrettably, the photographer went unexpectedly underwater in front of athletes. Sara almost went over him with the paddle board. Because athlete safety and well-being were a prime concern of ours, we took our concerns to the organizers. It was unacceptable for the photographer to jump into the water in front of athletes without warning, as it could have caused serious injuries. Michelle requested that the organizers communicate our expectations to the photographer, as we would be reluctant to allow him to continue taking pictures of our athlete if his hazardous behaviors were repeated. We understood that photography is important in the context of triathlon competitions, but the safety and security of athletes had to come first.

DAY 1: OAHU ISLAND

I changed outfits in the parking lot and faced the 180 kilometers bike ride. Because we had visited the island prior, I knew about the course and the wind. There were many hills, and the wind was quite strong on the south coast.

Our planning the day before paid off as we were blessed to witness traffic due to construction work; taking this into consideration allowed us to plan ahead. In order to account for potential delays due to construction work, we filled the bottle holders with enough water and energy drinks to last until the crew caught up.

Later in the bike ride, a vehicle came close, forcing me to almost go off-road. I was shocked when I saw the photographer leaning halfway out of the passenger's side window to take pictures. It was a risky maneuver, and I knew that there was a chance that someone could get injured. It was important to protect myself and the other riders, so I contacted the crew chief and asked her to request that the main organizer of the event prevent the photographer from taking any more pictures of our crew. I recognized that it was a reoccurring risk, and I wanted to ensure that there were no injuries.

Because I had visited Oahu before the event, I knew there was a shop that made a banana and water sort of sorbet with mixed fruits. While I was in the last few kilometers of finishing the first iron distance, Michelle went to get two bowls of this fruit sorbet. I went back to the hotel room with both sorbets while the crew was setting up the inflatable massage boots; I had brought in my kit. This machine provided relief from the brutality I was inflicting on my body. I ate both delicacies while relaxing in the massage boots. I was not complaining about life at that point!

While I slowly drifted off to sleep, the crew was preparing for the following day.

Day 2: Oahu Island

To give more time for the competitors to finish the second iron-distance before their flight, the race director asked if all athletes would agree to an earlier start than previously planned. We all accepted even though this decision would severely impact our sleeping time. After all, one of the athletes came in a few minutes before the start of the second day. I was fortunate enough to get a few hours of rest, although I had expected far more when I first made my plans. We were still all cheerful at that point and making jokes. We all laughed when Shane clowned that I only had nine iron-distances left. This feat seemed an easy breeze!

As the cold Hawaiian morning air filled our lungs and the head torches lit up the path ahead of us, we began our journey toward the finish line of our last 42-kilometer run on Oahu. Despite the darkness and chill, we were all invigorated by the challenge ahead.

Unfortunately, my excitement soon turned to pain as I started to feel my feet swell with every step I took. The discomfort was like a heavy weight on my body, threatening to slow me down and prevent me from achieving my goal.

But I refused to let the pain drag me back. I kept going, pushing myself further and faster despite the agony in my feet. To my surprise, I managed to finish the marathon with the second-best time of the day, despite the difficulty I had encountered.

It was a beautiful morning, and the sun was just beginning to rise. I had gone through my first moment of pain in Epicdeca, and now I was ready for the next challenge. After changing into my gear in the parking lot of Ala Moana Beach, I set out to join my friends, the turtles, for a 3.8-kilometer swim. Sara was there to guide me with her paddle board as I began on this aquatic journey. As I swam, I was overwhelmed by the beauty of the sea and the power of my body to continue for a second day in a row.

After the swim, I hardened myself for the 180-kilometer cycle around the east coast of Oahu. I knew the road around the monstrous volcanic crater of Diamond Head was going to be a challenge. The winds were unrelenting as I pedaled around the tuff cone, and my determination was tested. But before we encountered any traffic, the crew filled my bottles as planned, and this gave me the sustenance to continue while the crew was obstructed.

Afterward, I had already started feeling fatigued, so I decided to take a brief nap in the van. We got the trunk open, moved around some of the equipment, and slept for less than 10 minutes. That was all I needed to give me the energy to get back on my bike and finish this section. My crew was amazed at my self-discipline, as I had already set a designated amount of rest that I wanted to take. They were impressed that I managed to make such a clear-headed decision even amid such a grueling race.

The Epicdeca was a challenge that demanded much of its athletes. With the second iron-distance making its first victim, it reminded us of all the harsh reality that few would finish. Despite this, there was still hope for those who could not continue. With the Epic5 members arriving on the fourth day, Epicdeca competitors had the option to drop out and restart their challenge as Epic5 finishers. This allowed everyone to rise to the challenge and continue their epic journey.

The second day of the competition would bring the first signs of emotional breakdown. One of the five remaining athletes felt overwhelmed, having cycled many more kilometers than anticipated due to a mistake in the directions from his crew. After reaching the finish line of his final stage, he threw his helmet on the ground in a moment of frustration and exhaustion. This moment encapsulated the physical and mental toughness required to complete such a grueling event.

The incident caused our team to stop and reflect on the greater purpose of the competition. It was not simply about finishing the race but about the relationships that were forming along the way and what was after the event. We had taken on a challenge together, and when some of us faltered, others stepped up to offer support and encouragement. We recognized that our strength was not defined by the outcome of the race but by how we chose to overcome the obstacles presented to us.

After a long second day of racing, it was time to make the mad dash to the airport before our flight departed. Half of our party was packing up all our luggage while the rest of us got ready for the flight. Meanwhile, I went to take a shower and appreciated the fact I was not one of those who suffered from frustration yet. Even if, due to lack of time, I had to skip out on getting frozen sorbets. We all arrived on time for the flight. I was grateful for my crew, who was carrying my passport and credit cards and took care of all the luggage. This allowed me to treasure the few minutes of sleep I had on the cold airport floor. Once aboard the small plane to Kauai, we were served a selection of beverages. To celebrate the completion of the second day, our crew delighted in some juice shots together. We all chuckled while Shane shouted that there were only eight more iron-distances left.

As we stepped off the plane, we were hit with a distinctive smell of fresh tropical air. The stars twinkled above us like a million tiny pinpoints of light in the night sky. We picked up our rental car and drove to our hotel. On the way, I fell asleep in the backseat. I awoke to find us parked outside the hotel, a magnificent building that was lit up like a palace. Its grandeur was breathtaking, and I could not believe I had the good fortune to stay here. We checked in late at night, but I was already wide awake with anticipation for the next day. As we entered our room and unpacked, I could not help but feel a sense of adventure. After getting into bed, I could not help but think about all that was to come. Although I was only going to be drifting off to sleep for a few hours, my mind was already spinning with possibilities.

Day 3: Kauai Island

As I woke up for the third Iron-distance triathlon, I realized that something was wrong with my body. I had a sense of dizziness, and my stomach was churning. I knew that I had to follow my plan of having a healthy breakfast and mustering the strength to reach the beach on time. Making my way to the beach with my fellow athletes, I still felt sick. While all other athletes were given the go-ahead to commence, I started to shake, and my vision blurred. I stayed on the beach, curled into a ball in pain. I felt like I was going to pass out. Despite my clear agony, our crew member Billy rejected the help of onlookers by telling them that I was fine. My belly was in pain, my body was on fire, and I had difficulty breathing. But I knew that I had to face this challenge and complete the race.

The crew chief, who was busy with other parts of the organization, finally showed up to assess the situation. She told me to get underway and that this sickness might pass while I swam. Without hesitation, I went into the water and pushed through the feelings of vomiting while battling the waves. My mouth was full of salt water, and I felt woozy the whole way. She was right, though; as soon as I started swimming, the pain and dizziness slowly faded away, and I started to feel more in control.

DAY 3: KAUAI ISLAND

Looking back, my over-exhaustion might have been the cause of that episode.

The bike mechanic had a difficult job throughout Epicdeca. Putting together and taking apart bicycles for all the athletes was no small task. This job had to be done accurately and quickly so that the athletes could continue their ride. The bike mechanic also had to stay focused, even in the face of tiredness, as they were responsible for ensuring the athletes' bikes were in proper working order. The general bike mechanic appointed by the organizer was a huge blessing, as it allowed the athletes and crew to concentrate on other aspects of their plans while knowing that their bikes were in safe and competent hands.

While I was in transition, I heard the news that the original bike mechanic had family commitments and would have to be replaced. Consequently, the photographer doubled down as one of the mechanics for the event. After this sudden change of bike mechanics and my previous issues with the photographer, I feared that my equipment would be at risk of being mishandled. Therefore, I acted quickly to call the bike shop in my hometown and verify that my seat positioning was accurate. Thankfully, they were able to confirm that the measurements were accurate. It was important to ensure the right height and positioning on my bike, as minor changes may have led to long-term issues and hindered performance.

I confidently embarked on my journey to the 180 km ride but quickly realized I had been given inaccurate directions. My bike computer was to blame and directed me down an alley that led to a bizarre U-turn. I contacted the crew, who, in the interim, was delayed in traffic, and they confirmed the error. By the time I figured out the directions had been wrong and got back on track, I had wasted an extra ninety minutes of cycling.

My energy had been depleted, and I felt a surge of disappointment washing over me. I stopped pedaling completely, laid on the side of the road, and, rather than cycling with negative emotions, allowed myself to breathe. I eventually pushed through with determination and redid the distance that I had mistakenly traveled.

The task of our mission was to reach the destination, but I decided that we would take a short break to properly thank those who had taken time out of their busy schedule to come and crew. After all, it would be a disservice to them if I failed to acknowledge that they were present and doing their best. We had already lost a significant amount of time due to the wrong turn, and I was determined not to allow that misfortune to ruin our relationship. So, I decided to take the initiative and buy everyone a meal. Making a brief pit stop, I reasoned, would not only result in an additional delay but also allow us to spend a few moments together as a team. I figured this would be an excellent chance to connect with my crew in person and have some much-needed refreshments. We stopped at a local café, and we enjoyed some turmeric shots, acai bowls with local fruits, and a smoothie. We bonded over our shared experiences and laughed as we talked about this unfortunate incident. I left feeling energized and ready to tackle the rest of the race. The pit stop provided us with a moment of respite, and I am glad we took the time to savor it.

As I cycled away from the café, I thought of how we had listened to Joe's wise words and taken care of each other first. This proved that our team was able to succeed together, even in a demanding situation. As we powered through the rest of the day, I was grateful that we had taken the time to enjoy this small adventure and create our unique experience. This approach of taking care of the team and doing pit stops may have decreased our time for sleep, but it enabled us to reconnect and find joy in our journey. After all, no one knew when we were going to be fortunate enough to set foot on these islands and spend time together again.

Because of all the delays, I got back to the hotel room in the middle of the night. After a brief one-on-one discussion with the crew chief, I had to make a decision, and it was not an easy one. She explained that, based on the current estimated finishing time, I would not be able to finish the run-on time and still have enough energy to continue with the following Iron-distance. She made arrangements with the organizers that if I would quit right now, I could have a good night's sleep and compete the following day with the contenders of Epic5.

I paused for a moment to consider the situation, my body weary with exhaustion and my mind trying to process all the information. I had already established in my mind that I would finish the Epicdeca and not the Epic5, so I decided to keep going. Even though it seemed impossible, I had no other choice. With a newfound determination, I changed my outfit for running and focused my mind on the task ahead.

My crew took care of the organization while I kept running, pushing through the fatigue and using this ultimatum as a motivation to keep going. Even though I had no idea what direction the course would take, I trusted that my crew was taking care of it and kept running with all my strength. After several kilometers of running in the dark, my crew caught up to me and told me it was not the right way. So, I ran back to the course, in a way thankful for the mistake, as it allowed me to use the negative emotions I felt as a motivator to continue.

With the course being largely on a golf course, we were confident that it was safe and away from traffic, helping to make sure our crew was as alert and ready as possible. We thought it would be wise to take any opportunity we could to rest, so the two crew members followed me in the supply vehicle, taking turns sleeping while I ran. Working in shifts proved beneficial, allowing us to make the most of our resources and have a more alert crew. My feet were so swollen that I would do one lap and then rotate them in a bucket of ice water to give me a few moments of relief. I took advantage of these minutes of pain relief to rest my eyes. I was strategic in how often I did this, ensuring that I would not be disqualified.

At the halfway point of the run, most parts of my body were aching, and I was in immense pain, but I kept pushing on. During this long multiday ultra-event, it would not be uncommon to encounter athletes who were so fatigued that they stopped running and were simply laying down on the course resting. One of those was a man who had passed out under a tree in the wet grass near the hotel. I checked up on him and offered to run with him for a bit if he was able to continue. With some encouragement, we were able to get him back on his feet and running alongside me. Our pace was slow, but we were

determined to get him to the finish line.

When we were running those large loops around the golf course, we took the time to observe our surroundings. We passed by a local bar and saw some people going to dance and have drinks. It was strange to see these two different worlds side by side, with the bar closing before I had finished the run.

I felt an immense sense of accomplishment when I finished the third Iron-distance. Despite the pain and exhaustion, there was a deep satisfaction that came from knowing I had persevered and pushed myself to the limits of my physical and mental capabilities. The other athlete and I hugged and went our separate ways. I took a cold shower to reduce the overall inflammation of my body. The bed that night felt like a reward, and I welcomed it with open arms. As the crew zipped up my massage boots, I hid my face with a pillow and wept in a mixture of pain and joy. I knew that the next day would bring more challenges, but for now, I had to enjoy the hour of sleep I was fortunate to get.

Day 4: Kauai Island

On the morning of the fourth iron-distance, the Epic5 athletes showed up for the first time, and there was an undeniable sense of excitement in the air. I could feel it throughout my body as I stepped out onto the beach and looked at the water, which had shifted to form giant waves. It was inspiring and a little intimidating. But most of all, it was funny to see the Epic5 athletes with the same anxious expressions on their faces as I am sure we all had when we first started our Epicdeca journey.

My first mistake at the event was not keeping a good eye on the photographer. He had made his way out to sea, and I had not anticipated that he would yet again be standing in the way of swimmers. We were all swimming in choppy waters, and I could see him moving around, trying to get the best shots. When I noticed he was getting too close to me, I decided it would be best to talk to him directly. So, without consulting with my crew chief or organizers, I called out to the photographer, "Move!" and then after he had moved out of the way, "Thank you!" It was a good call, but I could have avoided what was about to unfold if I had gone through my crew chief first.

As I finished the swim, I made my way to the beach in front of all the crews and some bystanders that were watching this athletic spectacle. One of the organizers came to me and asked me to show him my watch to confirm I had completed the full distance. He then started speaking to me in a stern voice that was both intimidating and threatening, warning me that it was the last time I would speak to event staff in such a demeaning way. I assumed that the photographer had gone to the main organizer and lied about my behavior. The organizer's tone was firm, and he made it clear that if he heard any other complaints about my attitude or conduct, I would be disqualified from Epicdeca.

I was taken aback by his unwarranted reaction and the fact that he had not even witnessed my behavior. I tried to explain my side of the story, but he was unrelenting. He knew a lot of event organizers and shouted that he would ensure they would be aware of my actions and prevent me from participating in any future Ultra-event. I explained to him that his behaviors were unprofessional and inappropriate. He should have been communicating with the crew chief instead of confronting the athlete during the race, as it was disrupting my performance. He doubled down by saying, "Do you hear me?" My crew stood there and watched all of it unfold. I told the race director I heard him and then walked away.

I was both angry and sad at the same time, knowing that I would have no support for this injustice and would have to only expel these emotions by continuing this event. But once I was back in the hotel room away from everyone's sight, I could no longer contain my emotions and ended up finding a different outlet. I punched walls, shoved furniture, and yelled out in anger. It was only after this display of aggression that I could finally calm down and reflect on what had happened. I decided to look at the situation from a distinct perspective; rather than feeling wronged and angry, I chose to be resilient in the face of injustice. I saw it as an opportunity to demonstrate perseverance and resilience in the face of adversity.

I took responsibility for my actions and did not let my emotions take over in front of everyone. I recognized that the organizers were just as tired and stressed out as everyone else, so I decided to rise above it and remain calm. This approach allowed me to be in control of my emotions and helped me stay positive when faced with an inconvenient situation. It was a reminder of the importance of taking ownership of my decisions and actions, no matter how hard the situation may have been.

After a calming and reinvigorating cold shower, I stepped out of the bathroom feeling more clear-headed. I had decided to take control of the situation, despite the circumstances. I refused to be a victim of this oppressive environment and instead chose to create my destiny. To my surprise, when I emerged from the bathroom, another athlete was in my hotel room alongside my crew. She informed us that she was leaving Epicdeca due to the pressure and expectations from the organizers.

I understood that this athlete was feeling overwhelmed, but I was not going to let that deter me from pressing on. I knew I had to use a triathlon to distract myself from the conditions and focus on the larger goal of completing this challenge. I looked at my crew and said, "Let's keep going." I hugged the other athlete and wished her luck, then went to change into my cycling gear. I was ready for the next challenge.

With determination, I grabbed my bike and led my crew out of the room. We had a long road ahead of us, and despite the grueling conditions, I was ready to tackle it. My crew followed me, fully knowing I was laser-focused on finishing the Epicdeca. With this newfound understanding, I decided to focus my energy on the triathlon. It was an opportunity to move past the unfair atmosphere and set myself up for success.

Even though the earlier interactions had not been pleasant for everyone, I decided to take a break and enjoy some of the stunning views around me. After cycling for a few hours, stopping for a break allowed me to savor an acai bowl with my crew at the local café. The beautiful surroundings allowed me to focus on the peacefulness of my current situation. In these moments, I was reminded of the importance of taking a step back and appreciating the trivial things in life.

As we navigated the cycling course, a growing sense of tension began to develop within our crew. With every passing hour, it became increasingly clear that our differences in both personalities and abilities were going to be a major factor in our success or failure. It was vital that we worked as a team, and while each individual had their strengths to contribute, it was also important that everyone be willing to listen to one another. Unfortunately, Michelle quickly noticed that Billy was not adhering to basic instructions or taking part in the plan. He was not attentive to the crew chief's directions and did not seem to understand the importance of certain tasks, like feeding the athlete on a downhill which could be dangerous.

Michelle kept reminding Billy of the importance of following the team plan and paying attention to details, but it seemed like her efforts were to no avail. She understood that Billy was not intentionally malicious, but he did need to be brought back into alignment with the team plan. He needed to understand that there were consequences for not following the plan and that it was his responsibility to listen to instructions. So, after much deliberation, Michelle finally decided to let it go, knowing that I had already been through a lot today.

But then, just when we thought things could not get any worse, it started to rain. It was a cold and wet evening full of dark clouds and thunder, yet we still had to keep going. The bike lamp would not charge, and we could not see anything in the darkness. With the great initiative, I took it upon myself to find an alternative solution and decided to use the headtorch that I had brought with me for the run. It was an inspired choice, giving us enough vision to navigate the course. I had to be extra careful and attentive in order to make it down the hill safely.

The rain added an element of intensity to the darkness but also a sense of calm as I navigated with excitement the twists and turns. The headtorch I was using for my bike gave off a bright light that made the night seem almost surreal. It was both beautiful and scary as I felt the cool rain on my face and heard the sound of water dripping off the trees. It was like I had no choice other than to make it, and the adrenaline kept my eyes wide open.

As I stepped out into the transition area, the night air was cool, and it stopped raining. I felt ready to take on the 42 kilometers run ahead. I remembered the plan from last night and knew that I could take a few minutes to rest my feet in a bucket of ice and water mixture after each lap. It was a good strategy, and I was determined to stick with it. With that, I set off on the first lap of the race.

After a few laps, I made my way back toward the transition area to rest and dip my feet. As I was resting for a few short minutes, I heard a strange sound. Billy had brought his harmonica and was playing "happy birthday" as a surprise. Although I knew it was a bit of a disruption to my few minutes of sleep, the gesture seemed thoughtful. It was a sweet act, and I could not help but smile despite the pain in my feet. I thanked him as he stopped playing and continued my next lap limping like a pirate due to the discomfort in my feet.

The next morning, I completed the run successfully. I had endured the pain and made it through to the finish line. My crew was there to congratulate me and immediately prepare for the flight in a few hours. In the meantime, I took a shower and lay in the massage boots for a few minutes. A wave of relief washed over me, but the pain had taken its toll on me. As I lay in the boots, I was filled with a mixture of emotions. I was grateful for my crew, who had supported me, and I was pleased with my accomplishment. But at the same time, I was overwhelmed with a feeling of sadness. A part of me felt like I had failed and was not able to finish the race as well as I had planned. I was too exhausted to do anything but cover my face with a pillow and fall into a deep sleep.

Day 5: Maui Island

A few minutes of sleep were all that I had before my crew woke me up. I was on Kauai Island, and the morning of the fifth iron-distance was upon us. My day started like every other morning. I would roll out of my inflatable massage boots in tears, praying that all the variables would be taken care of and that I would be blessed to continue this journey safely. Though, that morning was unlike any other challenge I had surmounted where I believed I was on the verge of confronting my breaking point. As I walked the aisle of my hotel room to the car, the tightness in my iliotibial (IT) bands were screaming. I had a gut feeling that this was not going to be a pleasurable birthday.

We were running late, and our flight to Maui Island was quickly approaching. The crew chief urged us to pick up the pace, but we needed to be smart about it. Time was of the essence, and I had to prioritize safety and health as well. Even though I was still able to make clear decisions, I could not take physical risks anymore. So, I had to rely on the team to make sure we reached our destination on time and make all the decisions for my physical needs.

Seeing the pain I was in and the slow pace I managed to reach, Sara took it upon herself to make sure that I made it onto the plane. She had the foresight to contact an airport employee and rent a wheelchair, which she then pushed all the way to my destination. I could hear people laughing and cameras taking pictures in the background. But I was too focused on getting to the gate in time rather than being worried about how people perceived me. We had achieved our goal of making the flight on time. As soon as my head hit the back of the seat, I fell into a deep sleep and did not wake up until we had landed.

We had made it to Maui Island. It was a beautiful sunny day, and the view felt like something straight out of a postcard. As we were getting off the plane, the crew chief suggested that we split up. Two crew members made their way to the luggage carousel, while two went directly toward the rental vehicle company.

I was left by myself with the only task of slowly walking over to the rendezvous point at the airport entrance. As I made my way through the crowd, still trying to make sense of everything that had happened in such a brief period, I could not help but feel a sense of accomplishment. Although the journey had been difficult, I thought it was now behind me, and I could finally relax.

I eventually made it to the rendezvous point, and I felt a sense of relief. As I was waiting, a few people were told by my crew that it was my birthday. Without hesitation, they began to give me their best wishes. Despite the physical pain and exhaustion, I could hardly enjoy any of it. Here I was, miles away from home, surrounded by people who did not even know me, and they were trying to make sure I had a special day. It would undoubtedly be a memorable one!

When the crew came back, I had no choice but to follow their instructions and make my way to the rental van. As soon as I sat in the car, Michelle was direct and unhesitating. She handed me a bag with all my swimming gear and said, "Put on your wetsuit; you are starting again in 20 minutes." At that moment, my mind seemed ready to go, but my body would not let me. I knew that my IT bands were going to be in pain. My thoughts raced as I tried to keep a level head, yet I remained focused and chose to take in the breathtaking sights before me.

The start of the day was full of anticipation as eight athletes geared up at Kamaole beach to face their challenges head-on. Four of them remained to take on the exhaustive Epicdeca, while the other four were in line to complete the harsh Epic5.

While everyone waited for the go-ahead from the race director, I slowly entered the water to stretch. With the gun starting from the organizer, we all surged forward into the sea, pushing ourselves to our limits. Me, I had chosen to swim without the use of my legs in an effort to reduce any further injuries.

DAY 5: MAUI ISLAND

Despite the pain in my shoulders and back, I had to utilize my upper body strength to make it through the swim and mentally check another box.

After a demanding swim, I finally made it back on land and took some much-needed time to recover. I was filled with emotions, yet still afraid to express any vulnerability. I felt as if I had to be strong for the crew and not show any weaknesses. Little did I know, they had all experienced the same emotions yet were able to reach out and ask for help from each other. As my race progressed, I was hit with waves of emotion and defeat. I had to rely on my inner strength and resilience to make it through the day. I remembered all the times I had been rejected, bullied, and forced to do things against my will and tried to use them to my advantage. Through these traumatic experiences, it seemed as if my life was preparing me for this moment — to be able to push through the pain and suffering, despite wanting to give up. I was no longer running away from my emotions but embracing them and learning to manage them.

The physical pain I experienced pales in comparison to the psychological suffering that came from this experience. The doubts and insecurities I had to face daily were more excruciating than anything else. I felt like a failure, unable to complete the task, and like I was never going to meet my goal.

As I kept pedaling, it seemed as though I had no one to turn to, and it felt like I was in a never-ending cycle of pain.

The fact that I had blisters on my feet three times in the same spots and one arm that could not grip my handlebar due to shoulder pain was an indication of the physiological stress that I was under. I felt like I had reached a point where there was no hope in sight, and it was difficult to maintain any kind of optimism.

Moreover, having developed a rash in the butt area, I quickly realized that this was not an ideal condition for riding my bike. The discomfort and pain were starting to affect my performance, and I was becoming increasingly frustrated. I knew that I needed to find a way to fix the problem, so I used some cream to help reduce the friction between my skin and the bib.

After pedaling for a few hours, I could not bare the pain and situation any longer. Even the mental games were not useful. Could it be that after years of racing in ultra events, I had finally reached my peak? As the idea of what I was going through was sinking in, I started crying heavy tears. I still did not want my crew to see me in this state. So, while they were ahead waiting for my next replenishment spot, I stopped, grabbed my phone, and contacted my coach. I let him know what I had undergone. Because

DAY 5: MAUI ISLAND

he had also raced multiday cycling events in the past, he knew exactly what I had experienced emotionally. As I was talking to him, I realized that I had been through the worst part of the event and that all I had to do was simply keep going. I sent a message to my dad before continuing, and I just pressed on. Despite being in physical pain and emotional exhaustion, I was determined to complete this iron-distance. I understood then that it is the most difficult moments in life that bring with them the greatest lessons and that there was a strength within me that refused to submit to the pain and fatigue.

Soon after my mental and physical setbacks, tragedy struck yet again in the form of a flat tire. This could have been a devastating blow, but I was determined to overcome every obstacle. My crew reacted quickly according to the plan, and we kept moving forward. We were not going to let a flat tire stop us from completing this epic journey. With the tire change and a renewed sense of determination, I kept cycling. Little did I know that not even twenty kilometers later, the second tire would pop. It felt like someone was sending me a message to stop, but I was not ready to give up yet. I had been through too much to give up now. My crew replaced the tire once again, and I pushed forward. When I finally reached the transition area, I knew that everything was going to be all right. In transition, I had to take a moment to pause and think about what lay ahead. Once again,

I prepared myself mentally and physically for the hours of pounding that was about to come.

After almost an hour in transition, I was out and on my way to the marathon. Even though I was behind most of the athletes, I kept running and pushing myself further. Eventually, I got closer and closer to one of the Epic5 athletes. As I was running alongside him, I got to know some of his stories. He was an athlete that had overcome incredible adversities.

One particular story that stood out was when he told me he had developed a blister under his foot the size of a baseball during the first iron-distance. He did not have any first aid knowledge, so he resorted to using duct tape all around his foot in order to keep the blister together. This seemed like a moment of desperation and creativity. He initially thought that it would be a great fix, but as he kept running, his foot became increasingly uncomfortable.

As I was listening to this athlete's story, my physical pain all of a sudden felt small in comparison. I was running on pure willpower and admiration for his incredible fortitude. After running together for a while, he shared with me that he was newly married and had agreed to use this event as a honeymoon for him and his wife. I could not believe it, but as we approached his crew vehicle, I could see his wife checking up on him and encouraging him to keep going. It was incredible to witness the kind of support and love that existed between them. I knew from that moment onwards that if they survived this test of endurance, nothing life could throw at them would be too tough. I felt humble as I kept running while he stopped for some refreshments.

I continued running and walking Maui Island when I stumbled upon a $20 bill on the ground. It was a fortuitous sight, but I had to decide what to do with it. I chose the path of compassion and generosity and gave it to the homeless person who happened to pass by. It was a small gesture of kindness, but I am sure it meant the world to him. As my suffering increased, the importance of money and wealth paled in comparison, and it felt as though they had no relevance to me. I kept focusing my attention on what mattered most, finishing the Epicdeca.

Shortly after, I was running in the dark when my eye caught a vehicle on the side of the road. As I got closer to it, I noticed its window was lowered, and at that moment, the driver waved an electric shocker in the air and shouted, "I am armed!" It was an unexpected birthday gift that I decided to decline. After all, I was not willing to do the bacon dance at my party. So, I simply switched sides of the street and moved away from the vehicle. Despite all the stress and busyness of the day, I was still able to complete my run-on time. I was excited to celebrate with my crew for a few minutes. After getting a much-needed shower at the hotel, I was able to sink into a deep and peaceful sleep. Despite the chaos of the day, it was still possible to make it work, and I felt a profound sense of satisfaction at having achieved my goal. Tomorrow would bring another day's challenges, but for now, I was content to relax and rest.

Day 6: Lanai Island

Because only half of us were allowed to make it to Lanai, we had to be very strategic about our plan for the expedition. Two crew members would fly directly to Molokai while two stayed behind to go to Lanai with the athlete. However, the crew members going to Lanai would have to leave by boat.

In the morning, as we were waiting for the ferry, I was able to snooze for a few minutes on the rocks. Even the sound of the waves and the chaos of the crews scrambling to organize their trip was not enough to disturb this small nap. At this point, my dad had not heard any news since the receipt of the previous day's message. Since he was concerned about the safety of his son, he messaged Michelle to ask if I would be okay. When Michelle approached me during the ferry ride, I could tell she was concerned. She asked me how everything was going and if I had been able to process my emotions. I told her that I was still managing everything, but I was feeling calmer and more in control.

I took the rest of the ferry trip to take a snooze, so Michelle, Billy, and I arrived refreshed and ready to explore what Lanai had to offer. The anticipation of what adventures this tropical paradise held in store energized us, each of us brimming with enthusiasm for the journey ahead. As I arrived at the pool and got

237

ready for my swim, I could not help but be impressed by the hospitality of the locals. One young man had taken it upon himself to offer us transportation from the parking lot to the swimming area. Even though I was not walking with crutches, he offered to help me.

Upon finishing the pool swim, I began to cycle the 180 km. I was struck by the island's small size. It quickly became apparent that we had to navigate over twenty-seven loops on one of the main roads. Fortunately, there was not a lot of traffic, allowing the local police to easily direct locals to different routes. While all the crews had set up camp at one end of the course, a kind local man had thoughtfully parked his truck on a small hill in the middle of the loops. As we passed by him, he would cheer and clap for every cyclist that went by.

After hours of witnessing this incredible display of dedication, I felt a deep sense of respect for the local man who had remained by his truck on the side of the road for the duration of this 180 km cycling feat. After speaking to the crew chief, I decided to give him something in recognition of his commitment and support. I handed him an Epicdeca shirt and some snacks and offered him to join us for the run this evening. His eyes lit up with joy, and he happily accepted.

On one of the loops, something seemed off. One of

our crew members was not engaged and appeared to be distracted enough not to follow any of the crew chief's demands. While I had noticed this in other sections of the challenge, I had not yet said anything. After taking a short nap in the car to think more clearly, I decided to find Michelle to talk to privately. I stopped her and mentioned that it could be beneficial for the team if we removed Billy.

It was a difficult decision, but it demonstrated the team's commitment to completing this challenge. We made sure that this person was taken care of and found a safe place to stay until it was time for him to return home. We also covered a hotel for him for the remainder of the week and made sure he had a flight home. Billy accepted the news of his firing with a sense of relief. He was finally getting to enjoy some time in Hawaii and do whatever he pleased without worrying about work or the event stresses. Michelle thanked him for being part of the crew and wished him well, making sure that he was all set for his next move. It was the best decision for Billy, and he knew it. He had been feeling tired and stressed out for a long time, and this was his chance to take a break and reset. He was grateful for the experience he had gained but even more appreciative of the much-needed break.

It is no surprise that an event such as the Epicdeca would be a challenging test of physical endurance and mental strength for everyone involved. Though it might have seemed less demanding for some athletes, there are still some who faced the unexpected. This was the case for one Epic5 athlete who, during the cycling portion, collapsed on the side of the road under the burning Hawaiian sun. His crew, including his newlywed wife, soon arrived to give him some water and shade. It was a heartbreaking moment to witness, yet a powerful example of the strength and resilience of this couple. While any honeymoon should be filled with joy and relaxation, this one was undoubtedly more challenging than the average.

It is said that to reach one's full potential, one must push beyond their limits. Unfortunately, in the case of a fellow Epicdeca athlete, he had reached far past his limitations. As an Ultra athlete, not only was it important to have physical endurance and strength, but also to prepare for any potential issues that may arise during the competition. To do so, most athletes train their digestive systems for months before a race. In this case, this particular athlete was unable to continue with the Epicdeca due to digestive issues, which might have been prevented with the proper training in nutrition and hydration. Despite the disappointment, there was still a sense of accomplishment in that he was able to finish more than the fifth iron-distance.

I finally completed all the cycling loops and reached the transition area to change for the run. Upon being informed about Lanai's planes' size limitations, I had to make a difficult decision. As my crew chief informed me, I had no choice but to ditch my extra nutrition, something that I was determined not to do. After all, proper nutrition is essential for endurance performance, and it is something I was not willing to compromise on.

However, I knew that I had ordered far more nutrition than necessary, and I had to be realistic about the situation. Michelle showed great resourcefulness in making sure our situation was not a total loss. Instead of just throwing it away and wasting a thousand dollars of nutrition, she found a way to donate it to kids in sports on Lanai Island. This was an act of creativity and generosity that I appreciated. I am glad she was able to be ingenious and think freely.

Michelle's ingenuity did not stop there. During the running loops, she placed my nutrition at a key location I could feed myself while she oversaw other logistical aspects of the event. This way, she was able to make donations to children while supporting me without needing an assistant.

The two locals who cheered us on earlier were a demonstration of the island's hospitality. We felt honored to have them take us up on our offer to run with us. They showed an incredible level of kindness, and it was truly inspiring to see. It is hard to put into words how much their enthusiasm and encouragement meant to me throughout the marathon. Even as our group grew increasingly exhausted from the grueling trek, they never lost their enthusiasm. Those strangers did not seem to understand how difficult it must have been for us to keep going. That night, as I laid my head onto a rock for a few moments of sleep, they simply looked after me like guardians. I was fortunate enough to have them join me on my running journey, providing the motivation I needed to push through and complete this section.

To maximize my efficiency and convenience, I took the step to only bring one pair of shorts and a hoody. By packing light, I had fewer belongings to worry about and manage, freeing me up to focus on the task at hand. It was a difficult feeling to be standing at the finish line in Lanai and knowing that my only pair of shorts and sweater had been stolen. It was disheartening to think that someone would take advantage of my situation. My journey with the sweater began when I was fortunate to receive one from two generous locals who had just run 42 km with me. At first, the sweater kept me warm during my travels. However, it quickly became much more than just a source of warmth. It was a symbol of hope.

I was so confident in my sense of style that I did not care what people thought. I believed in my choice of clothing, and I was comfortable in what I wore. In hindsight, it might have seemed strange to some observers, but I felt like a fashionable trendsetter. I was wearing the same outfit everywhere, a choice of sandals, a hoody, and underwear that I felt was cool in its way. Walking around with an ugly tan, burned lips, and looking like I had been run over by a truck. Regardless, I was pleased my choices never wavered, and my confidence allowed me to stand out.

Upon completion of the sixth iron-distance, I followed Michelle into our hotel room. Took a shower and fell asleep as soon as my head hit the pillow.

Day 7: Molokai Island

After a good two hours of sleep, Michelle and I headed to the airport. When we got to the airport, I quickly realized that I had to find a teammate who not only shared the same commitment and passion for triathlon but also had the kindness and compassion to help me in my time of need. I had to think fast. I was on an adventure, and, as always, time was against me.

While I pondered on this idea, I kept walking around the airport like a pirate who had just lost a leg. I slowly made my way in style — wearing nothing but my underwear, sweater, and sandals — to the airport gate. I finally found a comfortable spot on the floor of the airport. Laying there, I felt like Tom Hanks, who had been stranded on an island in the movie Castaway. I was surrounded by the hustle and bustle of this small airport, and while waiting for my flight, I dove into a deep sleep. My mind drifted away to a place where I had found my teammate and the adventures we would go on together.

But then, something unexpected happened. A crew member from a team that was already disqualified noticed my pain and quickly assessed the situation. He provided relief for my aching muscles by massaging my legs and giving me some much-needed rest. It was a gesture that I had never expected, and yet it provided some comfort on this otherwise long journey.

I was so tired that I did not even wake up to thank him. But I was so thankful for his kindness and compassion. I was eventually awakened by my crew chief, who was preparing for the upcoming race. I got to my feet and made my way onto the tarmac. At this point, I knew that this person could be an invaluable member of our team for the upcoming Big Island iron-distances. Nevertheless, for now, his dedication and compassion made him invaluable on that day.

Once we reached Molokai Island, one of the athletes was met with a misfortune. The airline had misplaced his bicycle. Fortunately, it was eventually located on Lanai's Island. For the athlete whose bicycle did not make it to the island, this was an unexpected challenge. But it was one he rose to. He completed the swim and then set off to run the course without his bike, undeterred by this sudden setback. When his bike finally arrived, he did not waste any time transitioning to the bike course. On that day, in particular, we could all see him give it his all to regain lost time.

I had heard a lot about these famous *Molokai Burgers*, and I was determined to find out whether they were as good as they were said to be. So, I sent my crew out to get some. When they returned with the burgers, I could see that they were nothing special and did not take a bite. But I could also see the disappointment on my crew's faces. They had made a bet with the organizers that I would break from my clean diet, and they had lost. So instead of giving in and eating the burgers, I told them that we could still go ahead with my plan. It turned out to be a great decision, as I stuck to my diet and managed to stay fit throughout the entire trip. The organizers may have bet that I would break, but in the end, I showed them that I was determined to stay with my plan.

During the Epicdeca, I had the opportunity to put my nutrition plan into action. I knew that I needed a quick burst of energy throughout the competition and did not want my system to store any food for prolonged periods. To achieve this goal, I adopted a vegan diet which was made up mainly of unprocessed fruits, vegetables, and cold smoothies.

By having a combination of fresh local fruits and vegetables, gels, and salt tablets, I was able to maintain a steady energy level throughout the whole event and metabolize food rapidly. What made this approach even more effective was discovering that frozen smoothies would cool down my core temperature and help me stay comfortable under the sun. I was able to stick to my plan, eating fruit bowls while riding my bicycle and even getting creative by eating cantaloupe and watermelon in the aero bars of my triathlon bike! It was a funny sight to see, but it allowed me to get the nourishment I needed without sacrificing time or safety.

During the Epicdeca, my training app showed I was burning, on average, an amazing 10,000 calories per day. All while knowing that the maximum average of human consumption tops at only 6,000. Although I was pushing myself to a level of extreme exercise, my body was not able to keep up with the demands. Even though I was aware that calorie counting should be based on quality more than quantity, my daily caloric deficit ranged beyond 4,000, and it soon became clear that this lifestyle was unsustainable. This eventually led me down a path where various parts of my body began failing beneath this intense load. It was an important reminder that no matter how hard we push ourselves physically or mentally, our bodies need fuel.

If I wanted to go the distance and tackle ultra-triathlons, then I needed to pay attention to what goes into fueling my body. I remembered that some athletes use a different strategy. Such as in the case of Joe Jaffe, who adopted an unusual diet of McDonald's and gas station pizza in his quest for success. Whereas an ultra-athlete champion, Carlos Pena favored Oreos washed down with beers. It often gets me wondering if this approach could encourage others to take up the sport. Meanwhile, to offset my lack of preparation for the Epicdeca, I realized that a clean diet gave me more chances at success than any indulgence. Hence why I did not eat the burgers or deviate from my planned diet.

On the bike course, the athletes had to deal with far more than just physical exhaustion. They were subjected to unthinkable violence and aggression on Molokai. One athlete reported that a local man was running after him with machetes, while another was almost pushed off the road by an oversized truck. Even more disturbingly, someone in a truck came close and threw their drink at me. He shined a bright light on my face, attempting to prevent me from cycling.

In another instance, a wire was placed in the middle of the road in an attempt to stop me from completing my ride. Fortunately, it snapped as the wire extended when my chest applied pressure before I could suffer any severe injury. However, these incidents demonstrated the lengths some people were willing to go to prevent us from succeeding.

Due to the strict policy of not following an athlete, crews were unable to respond quickly in these dangerous situations. If crews were found to be directly following an athlete, the contestant would automatically be disqualified. It is clear that this treatment of athletes was unacceptable. So, we decided as a crew to take matters into our hands and protect the athlete. We made sure the crew vehicle would stay a respectful distance behind me, acting as a guardian angel and notifying event officials if we saw any malicious acts. I had already invested so much of my time and energy in the event. I was determined to see it through, but not at the cost of my life.

When I reached the transition area in the hotel parking lot, I was taken aback by the presence of a small group of locals chanting religious phrases. I felt a sense of awe at their unwavering faith to remove us. Unphased by this spectacle, I focused on the challenge ahead and set off on my run on the dark night of Molokai Island.

As I went on with the running section, I noticed that more people in the community were not welcoming to outsiders. They had giant lawn signs expressing their dissatisfaction.

Additionally, the prearranged run course was on the main road with no streetlights, and our crew was unable to follow us, leaving the runners in a vulnerable position. This made me think twice about continuing with the run, as I felt unsafe. I had to decide whether I should stick with the challenge and risk encountering potentially hostile locals or turn back and lose my chance at finishing the run. Fortunately, I remembered that this run was not about following a certain route but about meeting the distance. I was able to find a solution to complete the challenge without having to put myself in harm's way. The organizers were understanding of the changes and found them to be a safer option. This situation also permitted Sara and Shane, who was crewing, to have one member sleep while another provided me with the necessary fuel. Our plan was simple; I would complete a loop of five hundred meters between my crew and another athlete's team at the host hotel. This was a busy area with constant lights and traffic from people on foot that would turn out to be the safest alternative.

In the end, this plan allowed me to continue with the challenge without compromising my safety. Still, this option had an unfortunate consequence in that it took me much longer to complete the challenge than originally planned. My watch was not showing the correct mileage every loop.

While I was on the run, I remembered that it was essential to stay one step ahead. I had just taken the difficult decision to fire a crew member, and although this was necessary for our journey, I had to be prepared for any potential consequences. Despite the tricky situation I had put myself in, I was determined to make sure Michelle had all the help she needed for the next iron-distance she was scheduled to crew. Fortunately, I was able to find Packo, who had previously massaged me at Lanai's airport. His willingness to crew with Michelle at the 8th Iron-distance race was a blessing, and I felt tremendously grateful for his readiness to join our crew.

After extra running mileage, my watch eventually showed that I had run 42 km, and the organizers were satisfied. I learned an important lesson from my experience that day. It is better to have several devices for measuring distances. From this day forward, we planned to have two watches for the remaining running portions.

Day 8: The Big Island (Kona)

Our crew arrived early morning at the Molokai airport with a sense of anticipation and optimism that we might be able to finish the Epicdeca. Despite the lengthy delays and questioning at the airport security, I was still amused by the process of verifying each carry-on item. My crew may have lived in this situation at every airport since the start of the Epicdeca, but for me, this was the first time I experienced something like that. It was not until the security officer heard my story and saw the evidence in my bags that he realized the truth. I had just completed seven iron-distances on five islands, and I was on my way to completing three more on the Big Island.

The amazement in the officer's eyes of our previous week was unmistakable. The process of verifying my carry-on items, which had just taken several minutes, suddenly made sense. I could even see the fascination and million questions on his face about something he had never seen before. To him, it seemed like an impossible story, and we were blessed that he allowed us to keep going despite having such a farfetched story.

After disembarking from the plane on the Big Island, our crew split up to obtain the rental cars needed for our excursion. With no other option, I found myself in a car with another team. It was when I reached for the door handle that disaster struck. The crew member from the other team suddenly closed the door on my hand, smashing it in between the door and the doorframe. I could see the blood coming out, but strangely enough, I could not feel any pain.

My finger was bent at an unnatural angle, and there was blood all around, yet I could not feel anything. Not thinking much of this lack of pain, I wiped the blood from my hands into some napkins and applied some band-aids to cover my wound. Meanwhile, the crew member apologized profusely, but the damage had already been done. On the drive to Kona, I gazed at the gorgeous sights the island had to offer.

We had to be smart and prepared for this swim, as any miscalculation or further injury could have resulted in disqualification.

Fortunately, no one told the organizer about my hand injury. As we entered the water, we were joined by some dolphins who seemed to take delight in jumping around us as we swam. It appears they were present to welcome and encourage us to continue. The sight of these graceful and intelligent creatures was quite humbling, and I felt a deep sense of respect for them.

Because I had heard stories about the intense heat of the lava fields we were about to navigate, I knew that this bike course would bring its own challenge. So, after the swim, I sent the crew to a smoothie shop nearby to fill up the cooler with some frozen green juice. It was a gamble because I knew it would accelerate my digestive process, but it paid off as I was able to keep a decent core temperature.

We were wise to anticipate the scorching heat we faced. All of us were tired and drained from lack of sleep, making the heat that much more unbearable. Amid exhaustion, one of the Epic5 athletes fainted and fell off his bike on the side of the King Kamehameha Highway. Because this incident occurred before my eyes and far away from his crew, I called for my crew to stop and tend to him. I took charge, and one of us was sent to redirect traffic while another contacted the event doctor for assistance. Michelle, who was a nurse, made sure his vitals were taken care of.

The bystander who had stopped to help asked me if I was his teammate, to which I replied no. Even though we were competing in an event and a race to the finish, we all realized that the life of my friend and competitor was much more important than any medal. The sense of respect, camaraderie, and community amongst the ultra-athletes was what made this event so special. We were all there to push our boundaries and to show what we were made of, but at the same time, looking out for one another.

As the situation unfolded, one of the event organizers who was passing by rushed to the scene. This individual stepped up as the leader, taking control of the situation and ensuring that everyone was as safe as possible. I climbed on my bike to continue my journey.

When I arrived in transition, I was greeted by Packo, who had come to massage me. Packo made sure that he gave me the best possible massage, taking his time and making sure I was comfortable. The massage was like a soothing balm to my fatigued limbs, and I felt an almost immediate improvement in my performance after receiving it.

With newfound energy, I ran a few kilometers without pain. Although the pain returned shortly after, I still managed to push through and run until my legs could no longer keep up. After that, I walked and jogged until the end of the race.

Day 9: The Big Island (Kona)

On the morning of the 9th Iron-distance, I woke up late, and the consequences of being eliminated from the triathlon were dire. I knew that I had to get to the start line by any means necessary, even if that meant running in the streets in my underwear. I was not embarrassed because, over the course of this event, it became my daily attire. Thankfully, I made it to the start line a few minutes before being eliminated.

After the start of the race had begun, I knew that I needed to take a moment for myself and get ready. So, I returned to my car and quickly put on my wetsuit and goggles. When I felt ready, I went back to the start line, even though everyone had already commenced their swim.

During the swim, I knew that I was not pushing my body and mind to the absolute limit. I was exercising caution, knowing that if I pushed too hard, it could have a detrimental effect on my overall performance. My focus was on optimizing my performance, and I knew that excessive strain would not be beneficial. This is why I chose to take it easy on the swims, bike, and runs. This would ensure that I was giving my body ample time to rest and recover even during the event. While it may not have been the optimal approach for achieving top results, it was a wonderful way to ensure that I could perform at my best over the long term.

After the swim, I started cycling on the same course as the day before. During the bike ride, I remembered the lessons I had learned throughout the event: the importance of proper preparation, attention to detail, and focus on completing each task. I found myself reminiscing about how I had prepared for the worst. I had so many extra items that even the event's bike mechanic had to dip into my bag of extra supplies to help out those who had not been as prepared. By doing this, I was able to help my fellow competitors finish the challenge.

As I was cycling, I was surprised to notice one of the Epicdeca athletes running on the cycling course without his crew or his bike. After inquiring as to what had happened, I learned that he had a flat tire and his team was searching for supplies. Without hesitation, my crew and I offered our spare parts to him and his team. After giving us the supplies, we continued cycling down the path, and soon enough, we saw the athlete jump back on his bike and ride ahead of us.

I was glad that my foresight and planning had paid off because I was prepared for most unfortunate events and only had two flat tires. However, I had spoken too soon. Toward the end of my ride, one of my tires deflated, and we quickly did a tire swap.

Despite the unexpected setback, I was able to finish the cycling portion and make it back in time for the run.

While changing for the run, my crew chief came to me with a seemingly impossible problem. She did not know who was going to crew for me the next day. I knew that I wanted Packo and Myriam to join us. So, before changing into my gear, I called up the athlete they had come with. When I asked if Packo and Myriam could help crew the 10th Ironman, she told me that it was up to her crew to decide.

Thankfully, Packo and Myriam agreed without hesitation. I was relieved to have them join us for this monumental moment. With the help of Packo's massage, I was confident I would be able to complete the final iron-distance with strength and less discomfort.

After setting off on this before the last marathon, I was determined to finish despite the physical pain. I knew that I had to find a way to make it through, so I decided to take the insoles out of my shoes and extend the shoelaces. Even after all these changes, my shoes were still tight. Despite the discomfort of each step, I kept pushing forward and never gave up. After all, I was so close to the end.

For the most part, the 9th Iron-distance was uneventful. We swam, biked, and ran according to the same course that had been established the day before. The event proceeded without any major disturbances or changes. This can sometimes be the best-case scenario, as it allows me to focus on the task at hand and, in a way, take a break from the extra drama.

Day 10: The Big Island (Kona)

Because we did not have any travel arrangements between the 9th and the 10th iron-distance, the organizers decided to delay the start of the competition by two hours. This decision turned out to be a mistake. The wind picked up, making the water choppy and difficult to swim in. This was unexpected, but it served as a reminder that even the best of plans can be disrupted by factors beyond our control.

Moreover, when I was getting ready to go for the swim, someone started insulting me right before I got in the water. Though the person attacking me had hurtful words, I was determined not to let it affect my performance. After all, that person's opinion was only one of many and did not define who I was. It was more important to focus my energy on the swim ahead. I took a deep breath and stepped into the water, ready to push my body to its limits.

Despite the difficult conditions, my team and I stuck to our plan. We remained focused on the goal ahead and never lost sight of our commitment to excellence. The swim was not easy, but we did not waver. The wind was so strong that it blew another team ashore, but even in the face of adversity, we did not give up.

DAY 10: THE BIG ISLAND (KONA)

I was strong-minded to finish this race, and I knew that it would take more than a safety boat with an event organizer to stop me. Although we were still making headway and on track, the boat came over to get us out. I asked Sara if she wanted to keep paddling. Then with a hint of warrior attitude in her voice, she replied without missing a beat, "Heck Yeah!" With a focused boldness, I asked the organizer if we could keep going and finish the swim. To my surprise, he agreed, and so the paddler and I kept on our way.

Immediately after the safety boat left, a sudden mix of wind and waves sent Sara flying in the air. I was sure she would not get back up again when I swam over to help. But I underestimated her strength and determination, which soon became evident as she retrieved her paddle and got back on the board, ready to tackle the waves again.

I can still remember her yelling, "Let's finish this thing!" with a confidence that made me laugh. It was clear she was ready to battle whatever the sea threw at her.

In transition, Packo and Myriam joined us with enthusiasm and excitement. Once I got out of my wetsuit, they prepared the nutrition and gave me a pre-race massage. Packo's massage was intense, but it was exactly what I needed to relieve the pain from ten long days of racing.

I started my cycling journey full of excitement, knowing that this would be the last time I would cycle this course. At the same time as I pedaled along the King Kamehameha highway, my crew chief suddenly stopped me. She had just received a text message from the main event organizer, informing us that they had proof that I allegedly had stopped on the side of the highway to urinate. The organizer deliberated whether to disqualify me or allow me to continue. She also mentioned that I was facing nudity charges because of this incident.

In response, I simply laughed and decided to continue with the race without worrying about it. It was quite amusing, and I could not help but chuckle at the thought of being charged with a nudity violation for allegedly relieving myself in the middle of nowhere. Considering the fact that there were no predetermined locations to perform bodily functions, it was quite funny that someone would even assume that it could be a crime.

Whilst cycling, I could not help but laugh at the idea that someone would consider disqualifying anyone for such a benign situation. After all, I was only a few short hours from being one of three athletes worldwide making history. While I continued my journey, I realized that everyone, including the organizer, was just as exhausted from the grueling race. Mistakes were bound to happen, and I am sure that there was a reasonable explanation for this one. Sure enough, once we made it to transition, an organizer came to inform us that I was clear to continue. Though I was relieved to hear that no charges would be laid, I knew the race was not over yet.

Before running, I took a moment to contemplate the challenge ahead of me. I knew that waiting until sunrise to cross the finish line would allow everyone to have a good night's sleep, and the pictures would be better. By setting an exact time for myself to cross the finish line, I was taking responsibility for my success and ensuring that no one would have to wait up all night for me. I made known my wishes to the organizers so they could relay the information to everyone, and now it was time to run.

That night, I visualized myself crossing the finish line with a sense of accomplishment. This thought energized me and kept me moving forward. I remember the crew and I kept making jokes and laughing at all the eventful challenges we had been through in the last 10 days. We could not believe it was already over. When I finally reached the finish line at night and showed the organizer my watch with the mileage completed, I could feel my hard work paying off. The crew was delighted and immediately staged a fake finish line. While waiting for everyone to wake up to the predetermined official finishing time, we gathered in the back of the rental truck to commemorate our accomplishment. We sat together, sharing stories and laughter as we ate some of the fruits, we had brought with us. After a few hours of celebrating, it was time for us to formally end the challenge by taking some finisher pictures with everyone. We took turns getting photographed with the official banner, and all agreed that this was truly an unforgettable experience.

Post EPICDECA Story

The morning following the end of the Epicdeca, I awoke after having a much-needed restful sleep. I felt refreshed and delighted to be enjoying the first moments of accomplishment in a journey that had been one of the most physically demanding experiences I have ever undertaken. Accompanied by my crew, I walked to the award ceremony brunch that was taking place at the local restaurant by the water.

As I entered the restaurant, I could feel a special atmosphere in the air. There was a total of eight athletes present with their crew. Three Epic5 originals, two athletes who became Epic5 finishers after making the switch between the Epicdeca and the Epic5 halfway through the event, and finally, three Epicdeca finishers.

It was a special moment for all of us, one that evoked mixed emotions. On the one hand, we had the joy of accomplishment and, on the other, a feeling of loss due to all that was sacrificed to get to this moment. I could sense the tension in the room; it felt as though we were all putting on a brave face and trying to be strong.

As I looked around the room, it was not just our physical exhaustion that was on display but also the psychological and emotional toll of our shared journey. We had all pushed our limits, and it was now time to disconnect from this experience and move forward.

We completed the brunch with speeches, and then it was time to award our medals. It was an incredible feeling, one which I was not able to fully appreciate at the moment due to all of the emotions that were swirling around me at the time. After everyone had their say and we all received our awards, I went to get some dessert with my crew.

Packo, who had been a pillar of strength throughout the entire event and had seen me through to its finish, told us he was going to take on his first big challenge in the form of an Ultraman race later that year. As he spoke about his goal, I noticed that his face was solemn; it was not the same kind of enthusiasm that accompanied him during the Epicdeca. I asked him what was wrong, and he told me that he did not have enough money to buy a wetsuit for the race.

This was the moment when I decided to jump in and offer my current wetsuit, which I had bought only two months prior in Texas and had used for only twelve Iron-distance races.

When I proposed the idea, Packo looked at me with incredulity and asked if the wetsuit was really new after all of this racing. We all laughed as he quickly finished his sweets so that we could go back to the hotel and try on the wetsuit. Fortunately, it was a perfect fit for him, and from that moment onwards, our friendship grew ever stronger.

That night we waved ourselves goodbye, each of us filled with a warm feeling of kinship. Though we had only met a few weeks prior, I knew that our friendship was just beginning and would last a lifetime. We parted ways in the hope that we would see each other soon, and my crew left the island shortly after.

As I watched their plane leave, I was thrown into a place of solitude, which I had begun to dread. This was the biggest challenge yet — being alone with my thoughts and reflecting on what had happened over the past months.

Despite the beauty of Hawaii, my loneliness was overwhelming. I had spent the past couple of weeks in deep pain in front of everyone, and now I was all alone. This loneliness felt like a void, an abyss that had to be filled with something. I knew I could no longer find solace in the physical activities I enjoyed. Due to the pain in my body, cycling, running, and even swimming was no longer available to me. Furthermore, my crew had left and were no longer shackled to take care of an athlete. Even with my taste buds intact, I could no longer find comfort in the food I used to eat. Music had become a distant echo. Texts and emails had become unbearable to read, no longer able to bring me joy. I could not feel anything! It was a strange sensation, almost as if I were removed from the physical realm and had been thrust into something new and unseen. I was no longer a part of the normal world, and instead, I had been transported to some alternate realm. It was here that I came to understand what had happened when my hand was crushed by the car door and was devoid of any pain. I was in my world, contemplating the reality of my situation.

I felt a deep sense of fear and uncertainty. I kept laying in my bed, reflecting on how my life had changed in the last few months. Bouncing from feeling like I was on top of the world to be completely overwhelmed by it. I was now alone in a hotel room, with the curtains shut and the lights off, feeling lost and confused.

In a moment of desperation, I took the most extreme action I could think of; I stepped into the shower and turned on the freezing water. I braced for the shock, but nothing happened; my body was numb to the coldness. Then I turned on the scorching hot water, and only my skin turned red. I could not feel anything. At that moment, I realized how numb I had become. Not only could I not feel the physical sensations around me, but my emotions were equally devoid of feeling. I needed to find a way to bring physical sensation back into my life. Thus, I decided to get a tattoo.

I ended up going to a local tattoo shop and told the store owner I wanted to have a full arm tattooed. He said that his afternoon was open, and he started to tattoo. He worked for over five hours with only two small breaks for him to go to the bathroom. I was amazed by his dedication and skills. However, I still could not feel anything. The shop owner also shared that he had never had such a sight in his thirty years of tattooing.

It was then that I realized that I had to learn how to relax. I was not used to being still and not having motion in my life. It felt uncomfortable, but I knew I had to try. So, I started by walking in the streets of Hawaii, taking in the sights, sounds, and smells. It is almost like I had to learn the power of simply being and not relying on physical activities as a coping mechanism.

It was a strange feeling, being alone. But what I did not realize then is that this moment would be the start of an incredible journey of self-discovery. A brief phone call from my dad was the first indication that I was not alone on this journey. He exemplified that regardless of the magnitude of my achievements, I was still highly esteemed and valued.

The reality of this lonely situation came to me in a harsh but necessary way. I had expected that I would be celebrated and praised for my accomplishment, only to be met with the cold silence of reality and a short phone call from my father. I had naively assumed that the world would come to my doorstep when, in fact, I had not even taken the time to build a platform and a community around this exploit.

In a brief time, I had to learn that success does not come easy and that humility is an essential part of the equation. It dawned on me at that moment that accomplishment is not gained solely through luck but from hard work and commitment.

Instead of allowing the pain of solitude to destroy me, I started to reflect on my experiences, and I began writing short notes on pieces of paper. Little snippets of thoughts gave me further insight into myself. Over time, the notes grew into longer, more detailed reflections. I wrote about my experiences in ways that allowed me to gain a better understanding of myself and my current lack of pain.

As I wrote more, I realized that my reflective writing was helping me to process and understand everything that had happened to get to this point. My notes were slowly turning into a book, something that I had never considered before.

HUNGER FOR MORE IN LIFE

Even though this situation quickly turned into another opportunity to wrestle with my thoughts, I stayed a few more days in Kona. I flew back to Texas and reconnected with friends I had made during my initial visit. I wanted to make the most of my time, so before going home to Canada, I sought advice from some of the old friends I had made who were actively involved in athletics.

We discussed Epicdeca and how much of a challenge it was, both mentally and physically. It was clear that I had the physical capabilities to take on a race again soon. However, my mental state was lacking. My friends suggested that I take a break from the physical demands of running and give my body time to properly recover before attempting another race. With the potential for long-term damage, if I did not follow their advice, it was difficult to ignore. I decided to heed the advice of my friends and take a much-needed break from racing every weekend.

Afterward, I returned to my home in Canada, feeling a little bit discouraged. Even though I had accomplished what I had intended to do and experienced something new and exciting, it still felt like I had achieved nothing.

It was foreign for me to think I had to sit still and allow my body to recover. Despite the clear warnings from my coach, I wanted to keep training. Coach Jeff was wise enough to know that exercising could help me process the difficult emotions of my experience and that mental health was more important than any physical goals. He reduced my workout load accordingly, recognizing the importance of allowing myself to heal and recover to further my progress.

Nevertheless, I was determined to continue with my usual workout routine and made sure that every day, I got up and pushed myself. My coach saw my determination and collaborated with me, guiding how best to approach the recovery process.

With no sensation in my body, it felt odd, but I was able to push through and complete the workouts without any difficulties. Though I was exhausted, I found a new strength in my ability to keep going despite the fatigue and lack of energy. I was blessed to have the support of Jeff at this moment as he was able to draw a balance between physical activity and mental well-being.

On my way to visit some friends in Montreal, I decided to go for a lake swim workout. It was my first time swimming in a cold-water environment in years, and I quickly realized that my body had become accustomed to warm temperatures. What surprised me was that I could not feel the initial shock of entering the lake due to my lack of sensation. However, even with the added insulation of my wetsuit, my body went into a state of hypothermia.

Instead of giving up and heading indoors, I chose to push through and see what my mind was capable of. I wanted to see if I could go beyond my comfort zone and tap into the strength, I used to complete the Epicdeca.

Marathon du Mont-Mégantic

Only three weeks after the Epicdeca and thinking I could regain sensation throughout my body, I registered for a marathon in the mountains. My goal was simple; pace two of my friends to complete this race. Little did they know that the task would be much harder than expected. Thinking nothing much of the race and the efforts required by those who make these events seem easy, my friends trained only a few times in the weeks leading up to the race. One of them even thought that his genetics rooted in athletics could easily take him to the finish line with minimal effort and training.

On the day we all gathered at the guesthouse, it quickly became obvious that the other two had not done their due diligence and were ill-prepared for what was to come. I was disappointed, but I had to take the lead and ensure that everyone was on the same page. After some careful instruction and guidance, they were able to understand that the Marathon du Mont-Mégantic was no easy project.

Though I was still in pain and discomfort from the previous event, I knew that it was my duty to help others finish the race.

Even if the distance seemed like an effortless task to me, the terrain appeared unforgiving. The mountains were steep and rocky, with slippery sections that could have caused some runners to resort to crawling. But I was determined to help my team, so I led them up the mountain with the same grit and determination which had carried me through similar events.

As we went on, I could sense the anticipation among my teammates. They had never experienced something like this, and it was clear they were at the limits of their physical and mental endurance. One of the guys had a nosebleed, blisters, and even back pain. It was their first experience, but this was nothing compared to what I had seen in the past.

Although it was not an ideal situation, I am glad that we were able to go through this adventure and successfully complete this event.

Sprint and Team Relay World Championship

For the following two weeks, I kept pushing myself to stay in shape for the World Championships. Even though running was an extremely challenging task, I kept completing the workouts until I could not continue.

I kept telling myself that if I could endure this, I would be able to restore sensation throughout my body. At the time, I was unaware of the reality of my condition, but I took comfort in the knowledge that I was doing something to challenge and improve my mental fitness, which helped me stay focused on achieving smaller distance events.

The Sprint and Team relay World Championship in Montreal became a momentous occasion for me. Not only was I competing at the highest level of the sport, but this would be the event where I would receive my first recognition as an Epicdeca finisher.

I was approached by this person who had heard of Epicdeca and was curious why I was competing in a sprint event. After all, the distances were so far apart from the Epicdeca, and there was not a lot of recovery time in between.

I explained to her that I chose this event as a way to challenge myself mentally and physically, even if it was on a smaller scale. We both knew that I was not competing for any prize, but I needed to continue racing to give myself a mental edge. I was aware that I risked consequences; however, the lack of emotions and physical pain was enough to keep me going.

She was so moved and inspired by my journey that she wanted to help me in any way possible. It was this exchange with a stranger that made me realize how far I had come and that I could use the Epicdeca to motivate others.

While I raced through the streets of Montreal, I recalled something that had been ingrained in me: be my own biggest fan. No matter how difficult things got, no matter how disheartening the situation, I had to be my own source of validation and encouragement. This was a tool that I found immensely valuable in completing the 750 meters swim in the old port basin, the 20 km of cycling through the streets of Montreal, and the 5 km of running along the bay.

The team relay was a fantastic opportunity to display the determination and tenacity of my fellow teammates. Everyone worked together with their own special skill sets and abilities, coming together to create a unified and powerful team. Although we did not come out with a podium, I was inspired by the commitments of my teammates and their dedication to doing their best for the team.

As we crossed the finish line, I could not help but be proud of everyone's accomplishments and their will to compete with a great attitude. But most of all, I was happy to share this experience with my new friends.

Canadaman

The following weekend, determined to push even

further the boundaries of my mental fortitude, I decided to face an Iron-distance event known as Canadaman.

This triathlon in the family of Xtreme Challenges seemed a formidable test of human endurance. A daunting swim in chilling open water, followed by punishing hills on the bike and a run that requires stamina, determination, and courage to complete. The challenge promised to push the boundaries of your capabilities, both physically and mentally. However, with everything I had already accomplished in the last few weeks, this would be nothing but another event.

The moment I asked my friend Felix to join me in crewing at the event, I knew it would be an adventure that we would never forget. We were both excited and nervous at the same time, as both of us were highly experienced in our respective fields.

Despite the physical challenge I was about to undertake, I knew that Felix would be there for me every step of the way. He had my back, no matter what happened. I took my time to ensure that I did not tire myself out or hurt any body parts, but Felix was always there to motivate and push me further.

Finally, after hours of exhaustion and what seemed like an endless journey, I reached the last hills. To my amazement, even though I could not feel any of my senses, I still managed to finish another event.

Triathlon of Alma

I had the privilege of returning to my hometown the next weekend to speak at their inaugural triathlon. At the event, I was struck by how far my journey had taken me. After competing in triathlons in many countries, I felt it was my duty to share this knowledge and the lessons I had learned. It was a necessary step for me to take to move forward, and I am glad I did.

As I embarked on my voyage to do this triathlon, my mission was clear. My aim was not merely to complete the triathlon but to serve as an example of what is possible when you push yourself beyond your perceived limitations. My goal was not to compete or compare myself but to inspire others to take on the challenge of setting and reaching ambitious goals. In this way, I was proud to be the last one to cross the finish line and be an example of perseverance and resilience.

I enjoyed taking my time and encouraging others on their journey as we swam, biked, and ran together. It was a privilege to be part of each person's success story. The experience was a powerful reminder that all it takes is the courage to challenge your limitations and the commitment to see them through.

Ironman Lake Placid

Unfortunately, I had already committed to the Ironman Lake Placid before the Epicdeca, and the pressure I felt was immense. With only two weeks away, it was a race against time and a battle of recovery to make sure I was prepared for the challenge. I was unsure if my body and mind would be able to sustain more amount of stress. Nevertheless, my physical and mental capacity was already in such paramount distress that I did not consider I had much to lose.

I had a growing feeling of desperation as I tried to connect with something meaningful. It seemed that no matter what I did, it was all in vain. I felt stuck in this void of nothingness, and my senses seemed to have shut off from the world. My efforts to find solace or purpose in these events seemed useless, as if my search was a waste of time. I had no idea how to approach the intense exhaustion that had taken over me. I scoured the web for answers, but it seemed as if knowledge of complete exhaustion was scarce.

It was then that I decided to speak with the other athletes and coaches who had experienced similar challenges. I figured they would have some advice or tips that could help me regain my energy and begin to feel refreshed faster. Hence why, before I undertook Ironman Lake Placid, I reached out to my friend, Carlos Pena.

Carlos was an experienced ultra-triathlete from Texas who had raced some of the longest events in the world. I knew he would be able to understand my struggles, and he told me that even he had never done as many races in a row as I did. He warned me that I needed to stop, or else I could reach a point of no return and experience immense mental, physical, and emotional fatigue.

It was the same message everyone was giving me, yet I felt like I was on a chase for this mysterious exercise that would get me out of my predicament. Everyone was only trying to help me by allowing me to make my own mistakes and learn from them.

So, driven by a dogged determination, I set off on an adventure to Lake Placid, New York. I had no way of knowing what awaited me on the other side of the border, but I was ready to take whatever it offered. To my surprise, I found an unexpected companion in my son. He decided to take on the Ironkid challenge, and I could feel a mixture of excitement and fear radiating from him.

We soon found ourselves at the starting line of his event, ready to start the Ironkid triathlon. It was a thrilling experience for us both, and I felt honored to witness my son's enthusiasm as well as his sense of accomplishment once he had finished the race. The smile on his face was a remarkable sight as he stood tall and gratified in the knowledge that he had achieved something remarkable.

On our way back to the hotel, I decided to surprise him with an Ironman cap. He was overjoyed and immediately put it on. It would function as a reminder of his accomplishments, and he wanted to share it with everyone. It was a touching moment for both of us and one that will remain in my memory forever.

Sure, it had only been nine weeks since I had completed the Epicdeca, but the unforgiving terrain of this course would eventually see my body and mind reach complete exhaustion.

It was another humbling yet enlightening experience. It reminded me that even if I could not hit my goal of finishing the bike event at a certain speed, it was important to keep going at my pace. Having completed Ironman Lake Placid, I made a promise to myself: it was time for me to take a small break and rest. After months of vigorous racing, I realized that my body and mind needed a reprieve.

Although I discovered through this process that there are ways to improve the rate of recovery, somehow, I had to understand that there is no miraculous pill for recovery, and I had to allow nature to take its course.

Florida (rest)

It was now time for me to evaluate how I would recharge. I had to learn how to rest rather than continually push myself beyond my limits. I had to prioritize my mental and physical health, as well as find a balance between the two. When I finally realized that rest was just as important as activity, I was able to find a healthier balance for myself. It took time and patience, but I eventually got to a place where I felt comfortable resting and not using physical activity as a way of coping with stress.

I could not help but feel discouraged and overwhelmed. I had gone to see my dad in Florida, hoping for a chance to spend quality time with him and my son. But instead, I found myself unable to do anything. Sitting on the beach and doing nothing was not how I wanted to spend my time with them. Despite the discouragement, I continued to rest in the water. It may not have been the ideal way to spend my time with my son, but it was a way to take care of myself and recharge.

One day, my son asked to go to a waterpark, and I agreed. We ended up going every day. It was the best thing that could have happened. My son splashed around in the water, and I had the chance to watch from afar. I was finally able to relax, knowing that he was safe and happy.

Mexico (Training)

After such a long racing period, four weeks off seemed like a long time. I was anxious to get back to training, but my coach knew for a long time that a break was essential. He reminded me that the days off were necessary and that I needed to learn how to rest properly.

During these four weeks' break from training, I took the time to reflect on my approach to the upcoming world championship. I had to accept that my body was not at peak performance, but I had to find a way to stay positive and motivated.

I decided to take a leap of faith by traveling to Mexico for some training. The experience of being in Mexico had a profound effect on me. I was able to leave the pain and blisters behind and take the time to appreciate the beauty of the place. I still experienced exhaustion, but at least I was able to move my body again. I immersed myself in the Mexican culture and was struck by the kindness and hospitality of the people I encountered. Their sense of joy, resilience, and humor in the face of adversity was truly inspiring.

The most rewarding experience of my travels to date has been the opportunity I had to fund and organize a race for the local families. It was an incredible experience to watch adults and children of all ages running alongside each other. The adults ran for ten kilometers while the kids ran a kilometer. It was a remarkable sight, watching the younger members of the community participating in a race they never thought they could finish.

Witnessing the joy and excitement on their faces as they crossed the finish line was a moment I will never forget. It was truly humbling to be able to run alongside them, and it reminded me of just how important it is to have access to these kinds of opportunities. It was an honor to be part of their experience, and I am thankful for the memories it created.

In spite of the extreme poverty that many of these families confronted and the lack of opportunities these athletes were facing, they still found joy and excitement in something as simple as a race. That experience will stay with me forever. I hope others can also be inspired to create similar opportunities and to show the same kindness and respect to those less fortunate.

Ironman 70.3 World Championship

Before the world championship, I was exhausted and still recovering. Despite this, I was determined to make the most of my preparation time and this trip to St-George, Utah. After flying into Las Vegas, I made my way to Utah. Before I knew it, the women's race was upon us. The day before the men's race, I cheered for the women as they were suffering from cold temperatures. It seemed as though; the men's race was going to be chilly, and I would have to take precautions to stay warm.

Drawing on my creative resources and friends' advice, I decided that a fluffy cow costume would be the perfect solution. It was an interesting choice, but it allowed me to remain warm and still have fun with it. When I arrived at the starting line, I had no idea what kind of reactions I would get.

To my surprise, I was met with admiration and respect from the other participants. It seemed that despite my unusual attire, they could sense the confidence I had gained from my experience wearing ridiculous outfits while in Hawaii. I stood at the edge of the lake, removed my costume to reveal my wetsuit, and waded into the water.

The next five hours were a blur. I swam, cycled, and ran my heart out until I reached the finish line. Despite the sudden temperature changes, exhaustion, and fatigue, I managed to complete the course without stopping once.

Completing the championship was an incredible accomplishment that showed me how the body can sustain so much pain and still recover. Despite not finishing with a podium, I felt a tremendous sense of gratification in pushing myself to the limits one more time.

Ultraman World Championship

Before heading back to Hawaii for an attempt at the Ultraman World Championship, I reached out to my friend Tim Wilkinson. As someone who had already done the Ultraman, I knew that he would have invaluable insights and advice on what it takes to complete this ultimate physical challenge. After several lengthy conversations, I was armed with the knowledge and confidence to tackle whatever came my way.

It was time to fly out. My two friends and I boarded the plane, ready to take on this intense event with whatever it had to offer. Our plan was for my dad to meet us on the island and be our trusty driver in the crew vehicle.

As I took my first steps on the beaches of Hawaii, I was fatigued by all that had happened. Still, I was overwhelmed with the joy of racing again. This particular race represented my first focal point to aim for an ultra-event. My journey to becoming an ultra-athlete had come full circle, and I was finally here for the Ultraman World Championship. Taking a deep breath, I looked to my right and saw the looks of awe on my dad's face and that of my friends. It was a remarkable sight, and I was so honored to be showing them the places I had been on the big island during the Epicdeca.

We all knew that this was a journey we had been preparing for months, and it felt surreal to be standing on the beach with them. I faced numerous challenges throughout my training for this race, but I was determined to make the most of it. I had come a long way since the three iron-distances I had completed during my Epicdeca only a few months prior. I had learned so much from that experience and the countless hours I had put in to reach this championship.

When we arrived at the athletic briefing banquet, I was taken aback. Rich Roll, the renowned ultra-endurance athlete and wellness advocate, was in attendance. He was the kind of person that I had heard so much about and yet never had the opportunity to interact with directly. I was filled with admiration for his accomplishments, as well as what he had done to help so many others.

We talked for a while, and I was struck by the kindness and humility that he displayed. Even though he had achieved so much, Rich remained grounded and modest. He noticed my enthusiasm and encouraged me to make the most of my life and always strive for excellence.

Seeing Shane and Sara again in Hawaii was another beautiful surprise. It brought a smile to my face to think that we were meeting once more at the same place where we had left off at the Epicdeca. Shane was there as an athlete, and Sara was part of his support crew. It was truly an inspirational reunion. They had both worked so hard to make it this far, and I knew that they would only keep achieving more as a couple.

The following day was the one I had been preparing for all along. All my training and hard work were about to be tested in this event I had always wanted to take part in. I felt prepared yet exhausted as I went to get my gear together for the challenge ahead of me. After all, I had raced in much worse conditions in the past year.

When I started the swim, I quickly noticed that something was off with my paddler. He was constantly making mistakes that I knew a seasoned paddler would not make. It turned out he had never been in a kayak before and was doing his best to keep up.

Despite this, I knew that I could not turn around or else risk getting swept away by the waves. The only option I had was to deal with the situation while remaining in the ocean. I chose to trust in his strength and commitment to lead me to the finish line. I realized that it was my fault for not verifying his skills before the event, so I remained calm and focused on swimming.

Although I knew he was doing his best, this situation placed us on an uncertain path, with waves crashing around us and threatening to take us off course. As the hours passed, my nutrition began to diminish, and I started to become increasingly ill. I swallowed a lot of salt water, and my energy faded proportionally to the amount of vomit leaving my body. Yet I pushed on, determined to finish what I had started. I kept going, and despite the wave's increased intensity, I stayed dedicated to my goal.

After almost six hours of swimming against the current, my destination finally appeared in sight. It was an incredible feeling of accomplishment, and I knew that I had made the right decision to trust in myself and my paddler. I had not given up on the swim. I had taken control of the situation and overcame all obstacles to reach the finish line of this ten kilometers swim.

However, I knew the battle was not over yet. I still had to cycle 144 kilometers toward the bottom of the island. As I stumbled out of the water, dehydrated and exhausted, I was pleased to have finally reached the transition area.

During this short break, I laid down on a towel and allowed more of my fuel to come out from my body on the ground. I had to find the courage and determination to continue despite this setback. I knew it would not be easy, but I also knew that if I did not continue and push through, I would live with the regret of not giving it my all. After a short minute of rest, I got on my bicycle and started pedaling.

On the bike, I had to manage my energy carefully, pushing through the pain and exhaustion as I raced against time. As the hours passed and the twelve hours cutoff time drew ever closer, I felt a heightened sense of urgency as I raced against both time and my physical limits. This meant that even the slightest misstep or delay could mean disqualification. I refused to succumb to the fatigue that wanted so desperately to defeat me and instead used it as fuel for my athletic endurance.

Against all odds, I kept pushing and striving for the finish line with an unforgiving mindset. I pushed my body to its limits as I inched closer and closer to the end. Ultimately, despite my best efforts and dedication, I was stopped ten kilometers away from the finish line by an official who told me that we had run out of time. It was heartbreaking to see my hard work go in vain, but I took solace in the fact that I had given it my all and pushed myself to the edge.

And thus, after four world championships and more than twelve iron-distance races throughout the year, I had finally reached the status of a Did Not

Finish (DNF) athlete. Even though I felt defeated, I had the satisfaction of knowing that even in this race, I had done my absolute best. Although it was not sufficient to complete the event, it was enough to prove to me that I had the courage and determination to push my body beyond its limits.

The experience of failing in front of my father and friends was devastating. It felt like a heavy weight had been placed on my chest, weighing down my every movement. I was embarrassed and ashamed that I had let my dad and friends down. Little did I know that this experience would be a valuable lesson on how to approach failures. I had to quickly realize that failure is part of life and should not be feared but embraced as an opportunity for growth.

I realized that it was not my lack of ability but the very narrow margin of error that had been my ultimate undoing. Even in my failure, I had already won by giving my all and pushing myself beyond my perceived capabilities. Ultimately, I had failed in the race but succeeded in life by learning a valuable lesson — that many times it is not the result but the journey itself that matters. From that point onward, I could look at my DNF status with satisfaction, knowing that despite the outcome, I had done my absolute best. And for this, I was incredibly pleased with my result. This unexpected end to our adventure also gave us the opportunity of spending quality time touring the island as a crew. We visited volcanoes, ate at local restaurants, and enjoyed hiking trails. We turned this racing adventure into a touring voyage which allowed us to appreciate the beauty and culture of the island in a much more meaningful way.

This unexpected twist of fate brought rewards and joy that I never expected. In the end, my DNF experience was not only a lesson in determination and perseverance but also a testament to the hidden rewards that taking risks and pushing boundaries can bring.

After an exhilarating race, it was time to celebrate everyone's achievements. Despite still being devastated by the news of not finishing this world championship, I had the honor of addressing the crowd at the athlete's banquet.

As I stood in front of the crowd, I took a deep breath and said that although I did not get the results I was hoping for, I still gave my all and had no regrets. I wanted to inspire everyone by showing that failure is not a roadblock but an opportunity to gain experience and grow. I expressed my deep gratitude for the opportunity to be part of such an incredible event. After we all said our goodbyes, the racing season was finally at its end. Though I have been through a difficult and humbling experience, the most important questions remain — will I have the courage to listen to my advice and be <u>hungry for more in my life</u>?

Epilogue

"Either through growth or victimization, discomfort transforms everyone."

~JD

Are you still hesitant to push yourself and explore something novel?

Do you still lack the ambition and drive necessary to succeed in life?

If so, then I hope this book has inspired you to gain the courage to break out of your comfort zone and reach for your dreams by challenging your fears and self-doubt.

Risk-taking

While I may not have any special superpowers, I do possess the courage to take risks. I understand that failure will always be a possibility, but I would rather face that possibility head-on than live with the regret of not trying at all. By taking risks, I can learn more about myself, my abilities, and my growth potential. I understand that failure is not the end of me; it is simply a means of learning and an opportunity for me to make better decisions in the future.

We must be willing to take risks, see life from a new perspective, and challenge the status quo. Only then can we make real progress and discover a higher level of fulfillment. Therefore, this book is not meant to be just another text that you read and forget. Instead, it is a guide to help you on your journey of self-improvement. I hope that by questioning the advice I offer; you can gain insight into yourself and uncover the potential for transformation.

Critical thinking

Over the years, I have also come to recognize the importance of critical thinking. With this skill, I can evaluate situations objectively and make informed decisions for myself. Likewise, you must actively seek out different angles and perspectives so that you can better understand your choices and make decisions that are right for you.

No matter how difficult it may be, never give in to the temptation of quitting. When times are tough, and you do not see any progress, remember that you are fighting for something bigger. Much like an Epicdeca, the results of your persistence may not be immediate, but they will come. You are setting yourself up for a brighter future, and you should never lose sight of that.

It is going to be difficult. You will be pushed to your breaking point, and it might seem easier to quit, but remember that you chose this because you know it is worth fighting for. Perseverance is a virtue, and it takes courage to keep going even when the outcome is uncertain. So, stay strong, trust the process, and take it one day at a time. Remember, the hunger mentality is key. If you keep fueling your body daily with healthy habits, and the right positive mindset, you can thrive at every level. Take advantage of the opportunities around you, listen to inspiring and motivating words, stay focused on your goal, and never give up. You can achieve greatness if you are willing to put in the smart work and push through any obstacles that come your way. Believe in yourself and trust that with the right attitude and effort, you will make it to the finish line.

Friends

When I look back on the Epicdeca, I am reminded of what counts most in life — that no matter what happens during a singular event, life goes on. In the heat of the moment, it may have seemed that all those races I was attending would define my success in life. Instead, it was how I chose to live every moment with the people that God had blessed me with as family for this brief moment. If you ever encounter these individuals, I urge you to recognize the incredible contributions they have made in helping this mission become successful.

It has not been an easy journey, and their efforts

should be celebrated and acknowledged. While we may disagree with some of their decisions, it is clear that without them, the success of this mission would not have been possible.

We must never forget the people around us who, by their kindness and generosity, have helped shape our lives and journeys. Gratitude is a powerful force, and a simple 'thank you' can make all the difference in the world. We should take a moment to reflect on those who have gone out of their way to support us and make a positive impact on our lives. Let us extend our thanks to them, for without them, we would not be the people we are today.

While on my journey, I encountered this Frenchman who had nicknamed me 'the alien' because of his view of my feats being out of this world. In a way, he had unknowingly identified something that I was striving for, which was to be unique. This encouraged me to further strive to be different than the rest. By breaking out of our comfort zones and challenging ourselves, we can discover something new and explore our world differently. So today, I encourage you to live in this world while implementing change. Be unique; embrace who you are and what makes you distinctive from the rest.

In short, be different, be the Alien among us!

The Destination

Invitation

If this book has ignited your ambition and left you feeling inspired, do not fear embarking on this journey alone and reach out to me and my team at hunger4more.com for guidance.

We are excited to hear about how this book has impacted your life and helped you reach the next level!

References

Chapter 2

Phillips, Shaun. *Fatigue in Sport and Exercise.* Routledge/Taylor & Francis Group, 2015.

Riegel, Peter S. (May–June 1981). "Athletic Records and Human Endurance". American Scientist. 69 (3): 285–290. PMID 7235349.

Sitko, Sebastian, et al. "Power Assessment in Road Cycling: A Narrative Review." *Sustainability*, vol. 12, no. 12, 2020, p. 5216., https://doi.org/10.3390/su12125216.

Wakayoshi, Kohji, et al. "Determination and Validity of Critical Velocity as an Index of Swimming Performance in the Competitive Swimmer." *European Journal of Applied Physiology and Occupational Physiology*, vol. 64, no. 2, 1992, pp.153–157. https://doi.org/10.1007/bf00717953.

Chapter 3

Brodal, Per. *The Central Nervous System.* Oxford University Press, 2016.

Norman, A. W., and Helen L. Henry. *Hormones.* Elsevier, 2015.

Chapter 4

Tietz Fundamentals of Clinical Chemistry and Molecular Diagnostics. Elsevier, 2019.

References

Chapter 5

Søberg, Susanna, and Elizabeth DeNoma. *Winter Swimming: The Nordic Way towards a Healthier and Happier Life*. MacLehose Press, 2022.

Wright, Janet. *Reflexology and Acupressure*. Hamlyn, 2008.

Chapter 6

Moorcroft, William H. *Understanding Sleep and Dreaming*. Springer, 2013.

Pictures credit
Front Cover

Oscar Compean: JD in Tangamanga park 1 in San Luis Potosi Mexico – October 2022

About the author

Packo: JD celebrating at the finish line of the Epicdeca in Kona Hawaii – May 2022

The beginning

JD Tremblay: Noah being pulled in a sled on the snow in Saint-Gedeon Quebec – February 2022

JD Tremblay: JD posing on the palm tree over water in Oahu Hawaii – May 2022

JD Tremblay: Noah being pulled in a sled on the

snow in Saint-Gedeon Quebec – March 2022

Mike Fartey: JD drinking a bottle at Nu'uana Pali lookout in Oahu Hawaii – May 2022

JD Tremblay: Makapu'u lookout in Oahu Hawaii – May 2022

Mike Fartey: JD drinking a bottle on a trail to Nu'uana Pali lookout in Oahu Hawaii - May 2022

JD Tremblay: JD on the dock at Huilua Pond in Oahu Hawaii – May 2022

Epicdeca journey

Michelle Buckowski: Group picture with Shane, Sara, Michelle, and JD at Nu'uana Pali lookout in Oahu Hawaii – May 2022

Michelle Buckowski: JD sleeping on the floor of an airport in Hawaii – May 2022

JD Tremblay: Shane, Sara, and JD eating during Epicdeca in Kauai Hawaii – May 2022

Michelle Buckowski: JD eating breakfast on the flight to Molokai Hawaii – May 2022

JD Tremblay: JD walking around at Lanai airport in Hawaii – May 2022

Michelle Buckowski: JD sleeping in the crew vehicle in Hawaii – May 2022

References

Michelle Buckowski: Sara and JD going for the swim portion at Ala Moana beach in Oahu Hawaii – May 2022

Michelle Buckowski: JD and his bike at Menehune fishpond overlook in Kauai Hawaii – May 2022

The Destination

Michelle Buckowski: Crew picture at Epicdeca final ceremony with Michelle, JD, Sara, Shane, Miriam, and Packo - May 2022.

JD Tremblay: Michel and JD at the Ultraman world championship in Kona Hawaii - November 2022

JD Tremblay: JD drinking from a precision fuel and hydration bottle at Tangamanga park 1 in San Luis Potosi Mexico - November 2022.

JD Tremblay: Noah and JD showing their medals at Ironman Lake Placid New York - July 2022

JD Tremblay: Michel, Packo, Oscar, and JD eating at the Ultraman world championship in Hawaii -November 2022

Back Cover

Oscar Compean: JD coming out of the water in Lac Megantic Quebec – June 2022

References

Oscar Compean: JD at Super Ovalo Potosino in San Luis Potosi Mexico – October 2022

Oscar Compean: JD running in Lac Megantic Quebec – June 2022

Made in the USA
Middletown, DE
07 April 2023

28298690R00179